Human Resource

Management

Rob Dransfield

Series Editor
Susan Grant
West Oxfordshire College

Heinemann Educational Publishers
Halley Court, Jordan Hill, Oxford OX2 8EJ
a division of Reed Educational & Professional Publishing Ltd

OXFORD   MELBOURNE   AUCKLAND
JOHANNESBURG   BLANTYRE   GABORONE
IBADAN   PORTSMOUTH (NH) USA   CHICAGO

Heinemann is a registered trademark of Reed Educational & Professional Publishing Ltd

British Library Cataloguing in Publication Data
A catalogue record for this book is available from the British Library

ISBN 0 435 33044 6

Typeset and illustrated by Wyvern 21 Ltd, Bristol
Printed and bound in Great Britain by Biddles Ltd, Guildford

Acknowledgements
The publishers would like to thank the following for permission to reproduce copyright
material: The Financial Times for the article on p.106; The Guardian for the article on
p.35; The Independent for the articles on p.83 and p.115; The Independent on Sunday for
the article on p.113; The Institute of Personnel and Development for the material in
Figure 17, p.86, and the material in Table 1, p.22, Table 2, p.23 and Table 3, p.24; The
International Labour Organisation for the data used in Table 4 on p.86; The IRS for the
table on p.116, using information taken from the Human Resource Management Journal;
The Labour Research Department for the material in Table A on p.26; The Office of
National Statistics for the material used in 'The Pay Gap' on p.104; UniFl for the material
on pp.39–40.

The publishers have made every effort to contact copyright holders. However, if any
material has been incorrectly acknowledged, the publishers would be pleased to correct this
at the earliest opportunity

Tel: 01865 888058 www.heinemann.co.uk

Contents

Preface

This is a new and innovative book on Human Resource
Management. Its main strength lies in explaining very clearly some
of the major developments in Human Resource Management which
have recently, and are still, occurring in companies throughout
Europe and the USA.

Its very lucid coverage includes different approaches to managing
people, the importance of human capital, recruitment, training,
performance management, employee relations and employment law.

The author Rob Dransfield is a well-known and respected writer
in the fields of business studies and economics. He is a senior
lecturer in Economics and Business Studies at The Nottingham Trent
University, and has wide experience in the areas of teaching,
examining and industry.

Susan Grant
Series Editor

Introduction

One of the most important qualities that a modern manager needs to have is to be able to work with, and to motivate, other people. To do this, the manager should be genuinely interested in others, which involves finding out about other people, what interests them, what drives them, what their aspirations are, and what they want to do with their lives. Without this understanding the manager will never be able fully to inspire or relate to the people with whom they work. Having found out about the aspirations of work colleagues and other employees, the successful manager will then seek to create the opportunities that will enable other members of the organisation to fulfil themselves.

This book considers the approaches that have been used in managing people in UK organisations in recent times.

Nowadays, the term 'Human Resource Management' (HRM) is used to refer to people management in organisations. However, as you will find out from reading this book, the term can be used in different ways. Some people use it to identify an approach which is genuinely concerned with helping an organisation's members to develop in a way which meets their needs as well as that of the organisation. Others use HRM as a cynical approach to grinding better performance out of employees.

During the 1990's most major organisations claimed to be driven by a Human Resource Management approach. Unfortunately, it was also a decade in which the most devastating cuts in the numbers employed in major UK industries took place. It is not surprising therefore that many employees were dubious about the humanitarian credentials of HRM. In the 1990's genuine people managers were seeking to create a two-way commitment process between the organisation and its people. This was hard in a decade of increasing flexibility of working practices requiring wide-scale changes in attitudes and approaches. In the first decade of the twenty-first century we will have to see whether HRM is able to gain wider credibility as a people-centred discipline.

This book examines the nature of Human Resource Management and approaches which have been used in the name of HRM to manage the people side of UK organisations. Students will need to read further, using the references recommended at the end of each chapter, as well as the various websites. In addition, students can keep up to date by seeking people related articles in newspapers such as the *Guardian* and *The Independent*, as well as reading articles in specialist journals such as *Human Resource Management Journal*, *Industrial Relations Journal* and *Bargaining Report*.

Chapter 1 identifies what is meant by Human Resource Management.

It shows how Human Resource Management has developed since the nineteenth century, and asks the question 'Is HRM a myth or a reality?'

Chapter 2 shows how approaches to managing people in the workplace have moved on from the top-down Fordist tradition, through to modern approaches which involve devolving power to front-line employees. It examines a number of theoretical ideas about the best ways of motivating employees.

Chapter 3 examines the changing context in which HRM initiatives take place. In particular it focuses on the way in which organisations are increasingly dependent on human capital as opposed to machinery. It looks at the notion of the 'new economy', which is driven by modern Information and Communications Technology and networks of links, and considers the relationship between the new economy and the flexible business.

Chapter 4 discusses the macro-planning process which medium and large organisations employ to match the supply and demand of labour through forward planning. It examines a range of internal and external considerations involved in forecasting the demand and supply of people with the right skills to do the required jobs. It also looks at a softer view of planning people-focused objectives in the organisation.

Chapter 5 examines a range of human resource development issues related to the employment procession in the organisation from recruitment and selection through to termination of employment. It shows how people-focused work is now seen as part of an integrated Human Resource Management philosophy rather than as a series of discrete operations.

Chapter 6 deals with the important topic of performance management. It looks at the relationship between the performance of the organisation and the performance of the constituent parts of the organisation, including individual performance. The important role appraisal plays in matching individual and organisational needs is discussed, and the importance of good communications in HRM is introduced.

Chapter 7 is concerned with employee relations and shows how these have altered and how HRM is based on a unitary or managerial approach to relationships within the organisation. It discusses whether the decline of trade unions may possibly have reached its low point, as unions begin to adopt new strategies in an environment which has become more supportive of union activity from 1997.

Chapter 8 examines important aspects of employment law and other legislation that impacts on the HRM issue. It focuses on changes in the law in the late 1990's and 2000.

The *Conclusion* asks some questions about the future prospects for HRM in the new century.

Chapter One

What is Human Resource Management?

'Only by satisfying the needs of the individual employee will the employer obtain the commitment to organisational objectives that is needed for organisational success, and only by contributing to organisational success will employees be able to satisfy their personal employment needs.'
Derek Torrington and Laura Hall

Human resources are the people that work for an **organisation**, and the contributions that they make through their **skills**, their **knowledge** and their **competence**. **Managing people** at work is concerned with devising plans and approaches which best support and enable an organisation's people to contribute effectively in helping the organisation to meet its objectives.

Definitions

Skills: An individual's ability to perform physical and mental tasks.
Knowledge: Information that an individual knows and uses.
Competence: The way an individual behaves when performing a job.

The importance of Human Resource Management
Today, effective **Human Resource Management** (HRM) is more important than it has ever been, because:

- People and their intelligence are the key resource of the **'knowledge-based economy'** (the modern economy in which highly qualified, highly skilled employees often working with Information and Communications Technology systems make a significant contribution to national output) in which 'intelligent organisations' (of which the prime example, is the US-based Microsoft) are the key drivers of economic growth in the global economy.
- People can, and frequently do change jobs. They can move from one organisation where they don't feel that their contribution is 'valued' to one where their efforts are recognised and rewarded.
- Managers at all levels within an organisation have a better understanding of Human Resource Management than in the past.

The development of modern HRM approaches

Approaches to managing people changed dramatically over the course of the twentieth century. At the start of the century wage **labour** was typically seen as a resource that needed to be tightly supervised and controlled, enabling command and control of effort and resultant output from above. In the Industrial System inherited from the nineteenth century employees actions were rigidly defined, and closely supervised by a supervisory class who were typically promoted from the **shopfloor**. In return for a wage, employees were expected to accept the work regime established by the management of the organisation.

The end of the nineteenth century saw the development of the roots of a more humane approach to managing people, among groups of enlightened employers such as Rowntree of York, Cadbury in Birmingham and Huntley and Palmer in Reading. The first **Industrial Welfare Officer** was Mary Wood who became the industrial welfare officer at Rowntree's in York in 1896 with responsibility for looking after the well-being of women and children in the workforce and to watch over their health and behaviour.

Welfare work in the early twentieth century was primarily of a paternalistic nature, and by 1913 Seebohm Rowntree (the philanthropic sweets and chocolate manufacturer) was able to organise a conference in York with 60 delegates. At this conference the Welfare Workers Association was formed which today has become the **Institute of Personnel and Development**, a professional body for Human Resource professionals.

Increasingly people management has developed as a key business responsibility, involving the recruitment and selection of employees, industrial relations work, mediating in disputes between employees and managers, taking responsibility for the implementation of legislation relating to people at work, and many other areas.

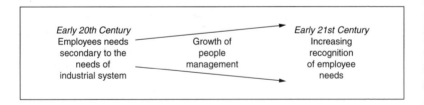

Empowerment

A major weakness of UK attitudes to managing people at work, which continues to exist in many organisations today, is that of manage-

HRM activities

Today, therefore, the key activities of HRM specialists typically include:

- creating the HRM plans and procedures for the whole organisation
- creating systems for the management of HRM
- recruitment and selection
- training and development
- workforce planning
- creation of employment contracts
- ensuring fair treatment of employees
- ensuring equal opportunities
- assessing the performance of employees
- managing employee welfare
- providing a counselling service for employees
- managing the payment and rewards system for employees
- supervising health and safety procedures
- disciplining individuals
- dealing with grievances
- dismissal
- redundancy
- negotiation
- ensuring the organisation's compliance with employment law
- encouraging employee involvement.

ment paternalism. In many organisations employees have been given little responsibility for decision making.

In a fast changing business environment this has left many companies at a disadvantage because they have failed to capitalise on the knowledge, inventiveness, and initiative of their people.

In the USA, companies began to wake up to the need for a new approach to managing human resources in the 1980s, as a result of the success of Japanese companies. Japanese industry had restructured after the Second World War, and had systematically introduced new 'quality based approaches'. These new approaches involve employees in the quality management process. **Quality Circles** are small teams of employees (including managers) who work together to come up with new ideas for improving work and performance. The Quality Circle approach, involves a great leap forward in thinking about the role of the human resource. Each team member's contribution is valued, leading to considerable improvements in motivation. The ground level employee is usually best placed to identify improvements that can be made to working practice in areas which they have direct experience of.

Japanese firms stressed the importance of 'kaizen' (continuous improvement) in the organisation, which should be driven by employees at every level in the organisation being given powers (using set procedures) to make improvements to the work that they are doing including the changing of business processes. Japan's Kaizen Institute defines kaizen as involving continual change in small steps, by involving those at the base of the organisation in conjunction with team leaders and line managers, encouraged by top management in the organisation.

In the 1970s and 1980s Japanese manufacturers made great inroads into Western markets forcing US companies to take stock. By the 1980s therefore the new concept of HRM was taking hold in the US before crossing the Atlantic to the UK.

In simple terms empowerment involves managers handing over power to make decisions to those best placed to make and implement intelligent decisions. **Grass roots** employees make very important decisions in their everyday lives. Many decide to buy a house, and arrange the mortgage repayments; most at some stage get married and raise a family; they organise their children's education, and arrange transport and household arrangements for the family; some play a prominent part in running sports clubs and voluntary societies. Most people manage these decisions and activities with considerable skill. It doesn't require a great leap of the imagination to realise that these decision making skills can be harnessed to the benefit of the organisation.

In the 1990s it became fashionable to use the term Human Resource Management to refer to situations in which organisations introduced systematic sets of policies and procedures for managing people at work based on the concept of **empowerment**. Typically the HRM approach would involve some or all of the following:

- **Delayering** organisations, away from tall, hierarchical structures, and towards, flatter more democratic structures.
- Changing the communication structure in the organisation away from a predominantly top-down pattern, to one in which there was a free flow of communications in a variety of directions – down-up, horizontal, diagonal, etc.
- Encouraging everyone to take more initiative for decision making.
- Introducing sets of new approaches including team briefings, appraisal systems, harmonisation of terms and conditions of work, quality circles, devolved management, empowerment, and so on.

Defining Human Resource Management

It is obvious that we are living in the age of Human Resource Management. However, there is considerable debate as to what HRM entails. The problem with the concept of HRM is that it is widely recognised as being a good thing. Most managers who deal with people at work claim to be human resource managers. However, studying the actions of these human resource managers reveals considerable differences in their approaches.

Study the literature of HRM and you will find an emphasis on four main areas:

1. That HRM is a strategic concern for the organisation.
2. That HRM involves decentralising people work to line managers.
3. That HRM involves a co-ordinated set of policies and activities.
4. That HRM involves identifying the needs and requirements of people in the workplace.

A strategic concern for the organisation

Business strategies are the key long-term plans which concern the whole of the organisation and its resources. Business strategies tend to be formulated by senior managers within the organisation. Today, most major organisations give a high priority to people management in their corporate **objectives** and plans. This is because **human capital** (the knowledge and experience of people) is the main source of adding value to an organisation's products.

In the 1980s companies rarely mentioned HRM as a major planning issue. In the first decade of the twenty-first century, there are very few companies that ignore human resources.

Because HRM is given strategic importance in the organisation this filters down to everything that the organisation does.

Decentralising people work to line managers

Until the 1990s most organisations had a specialist **personnel function** which principally took responsibility for all matters concerning people at work. Today, many aspects of people work have been decentralised. The modern HRM department is responsible for setting up people management systems, and for supporting line managers in managing their own human resources. For example, the human resource managers may create a system for advertising jobs, interviewing applicants for jobs and other work involved with recruitment and selection. However, individual line managers (in accounts, marketing, etc) will be responsible for carrying out their own recruitment activities with support from HRM specialists. Bank managers will train their own staff, often using packages designed by central HRM specialists, rather than sending staff to Head Office for specialist training (as was the case until recently).

The advantage of giving line managers responsibility for HRM is that it enables the HRM philosophy of valuing people to become part of everything the organisation does, rather than simply being part of the way of working of a few specialists in the organisation. By devolving HRM functions to line managers, they take on a people centred mindset which is part of the overall strategy of the organisation, while at the same time focusing on the technical aspects of task completion in their specialist areas.

HRM is a co-ordinated set of policies and activities

If HRM is to work in practice as well as in theory it needs to operate in a co-ordinated way across the organisation, rather than simply to exist in a fragmentary way within an organisation. Following on from the notion of HRM as strategy, then there is a need for co-ordination of HRM across the organisation which will normally be the responsibility of HRM specialists working with other influential managers.

Identifying the needs and requirements of people in the workplace

For HRM to be successful, then a two-way process needs to be created between the individual objectives of individual employees, and the objectives of the organisation (Figure 1).

All successful organisations communicate their objectives to every member of the organisation so that everyone is pulling in the same direction. However, if the organisation is to gain the commitment of its employees it must also find out about the personal development aspirations of the individuals that make up an organisation. The organisation that asks me what my personal aspirations are for next year, five years time, and in ten years, and then asks me how it can help me to develop to achieve these goals is likely to win my commitment. Most people want to develop themselves or to improve their working conditions. Some people are very ambitious, others are contented with very little. However, if they are going to commit themselves to the organisation they need to feel that the organisation is committed to them. A number of writers have therefore argued that a **'commitment' model** for the organisation will best be created by those organisations that value and prize their human resources.

Human Resource Management – myth or reality?

Much was written in the 1990s about the new world of HRM. Many

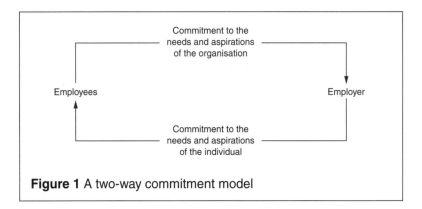

Figure 1 A two-way commitment model

organisations changed the title of their people specialists from 'personnel' to 'human resource' managers. The public relations literature of most major companies was awash with statements about 'people being our greatest resource', and the 'importance of meeting individual needs'.

However, the mid to late-1990s also gave rise to considerable cynicism about company intentions. While the people managers were talking up HRM most companies were engaged in a process of 'delayering' and 'downsizing', and were replacing full-time employees with part-time, flexible workers. Security of employment declined and many of those that remained in work felt increasing pressure to perform, leading to a rising incidence of stress related illness.

Cynics wondered whether HRM was just another way for organisations to sugar the pill of cost cutting. While those still in work benefited, for example, from being allowed to make more decisions, and being asked to outline their career aspirations during job appraisal, there was always the nagging doubt that at least in some companies HRM was not a wholehearted humanitarian measure.

This questioning of the real nature of HRM has led specialists to distinguish between two approaches to strategic HRM – a hard and a soft approach.

The **hard HRM** approach recognises people as the key organisational resource but with an 'instrumental approach'. It is seen that if you treat people better they will provide better results for 'you'. While the organisation makes statements about valuing its human resource the overall intention is to maximise other organisational returns such as profits and sales. This is a business-oriented approach to strategic management, and any such business would be expected to discard its people when they are seen as unnecessary costs.

The **soft HRM** approach also recognises people as a key organisational resource, but the emphasis is on nurturing and developing people because they are people. The qualitative difference is that the softer approach emphasises humanity, and it is based on the two-way commitment model. Believers in the soft approach would also argue that this will lead to higher business returns.

KEY WORDS

Human resources	Quality Circles
Organisation	Kaizen
Skills	Grass roots
Knowledge	Empowerment
Competence	Delayering
Managing people	Business strategies
Human Resource Management	Objectives
Knowledge-based economy	Human capital
Labour	Personnel function
Shopfloor	Commitment model
Industrial Welfare Officer	Hard HRM
Institute of Personnel and Development	Soft HRM

Further reading

Dransfield, R. *et al.*, Chapters 1 and 6 in *Human Resource Management for Higher Awards*, Heinemann, 1996.

Foot, M. and Hook, C., Chapter 1 in *Introducing Human Resource Management*, Longman, 1999.

Schermerhorn, J. R. *et al.*, Chapter 3 in *Managing Organisational Behaviour*, John Wiley, 2000.

Mabey, C. *et al.*, Chapter 1 in *Human Resource Management*, Blackwell Business, 1998.

Useful websites

Institute of Personnel and Development, the professional body that represents personnel and development professionals in the UK: www.ipd.co.uk

People Management, the journal produced for the IPD with articles relating to managing people at work: www.peoplemanagement. co.uk.

Essay topics
1. What do you understand by the term empowerment? [5 marks]
   What are the principal benefits of empowerment:
   (a) to individual employees [10 marks]
   (b) the organisation? [10 marks]
2. To what extent might Human Resource Management be seen as resulting from a response to external environmental pressures rather than as a philosophical choice of management? [25 marks]

Data response question

A new approach at GEC Marconi

GEC Marconi is a UK-based company which has had to adjust the way that it thinks and operates considerably from the 1990s onwards. As a result of the arrival of the 'Peace Dividend' (the breaking down of the East/West divide leading to a rapid run down in military forces and spending) the company suddenly found that it was no longer working with the security of Ministry of Defence contracts. Instead it was having to be far more competitive. This required the company to change working practices within the organisation in order to increase productivity. The way that this was carried out was through empowering the workforce.

Traditionally engineering workers had been told what to do, and had worked on specialised jobs – each specialist would take a job out of the work-in-progress store, add value to a designated job, and then return the product to the work-in-progress store. There was a top-down approach to relationships, ground level employees being told what to do. The net effect was that the workforce was not highly motivated and tended to blame other people when completed jobs did not meet required quality standards. In order to transform the company it was decided to transform working practices and organise employees into small self-managing teams (cells), each with responsibility for seeing jobs through from start to finish. The cells would research their own practice in order to identify improvements that they could make. This process was introduced over the period 1998–2000.

This transformation in approach to managing people and work has been a success. Initially there were few volunteers for the project; then when a pilot cell was created and was shown to be successful everyone wanted to buy into the new approach to working. Employees responded to a new way of working which unleashed the intelligence of all individuals. It is this step forward to the intelligent organisation and the recognition of the intelligent worker that has the potential to create world class companies.

1. How have employees at GEC-Marconi been empowered? [5 marks]
2. What are the positive benefits of this empowerment process? [5 marks]
3. Why do you think GEC-Marconi did not introduce the empowerment process earlier? [4 marks]
4. Why might (a) some managers, and (b) some employees, have been reluctant to get involved in the empowerment process? [6 marks]
5. How would the new approach to cell working require new types of:
   (a) skills
   (b) knowledge, and
   (c) competence? [6 marks]

Chapter Two

Changing perspectives on the role of people in the workplace

'*Do incentives work? The answer depends on what is meant by "work". Rewards, like punishments are extremely effective at producing one thing, and only one thing: temporary compliance. But carrots and sticks are strikingly ineffective at producing lasting change in attitudes or even in behaviours. They do not create an enduring commitment to any value or action, they merely and temporarily, change what we do.*'
Alfred Kohn

The twentieth century saw three major phases of thinking about ways of managing people and the role of the human resource:

1. **Fordism** and **scientific management**.
2. The **human relations** approach.
3. **Empowerment** based/HRM approaches.

Fordism and scientific management
Henry Ford
In the early years of the twentieth century, approaches to managing employees were radically different to those used by enlightened managers today. The first few decades of the twentieth century saw the creation of an industrial system in which machinery was seen as the predominant factor of production. Huge new industrial systems were created such as the Ford Motor Company (see box on page 14).

Taylor's scientific management
The best known exponent of scientific management in the early part of the twentieth century was Frederick Winslow Taylor. In his book, *The Principles of Scientific Management* (1911), Taylor set out that the role of the manager was to plan and control work and to give orders, while other employees were meant simply to carry out these orders. He believed that workers were only motivated by the prospect of earning money.

Taylor set out to find ways of maximising the efficiency of labour using the stopwatch and **'time and motion' studies**. He recorded the

Henry Ford

Henry Ford organised his company as a giant system for efficiently turning inputs into finished motor vehicles. His achievement was outstanding, in creating a technical system that produced millions of vehicles that could be afforded by the masses. The weakness of the system that he created was that the aspirations and needs of individual employees were subjugated to the industrial system. Labourers were simply factors of production that were rewarded for their efforts. Moreover, many of the car workers did not need to have any great level of skills. They merely acted as operatives working the production line carrying out routine operations.

Henry Ford was a farmer's son from Michigan. In his late twenties he decided to become a mechanic rather than a farmer. In 1898 he set up the Ford Motor Company with eleven associates. In 1908 the Model T, 'the car for the great multitude' was launched. By 1920 Ford had bought out his associates. The way Ford managed his car plants was strongly influenced by a belief that he could bring salvation and liberation to the world through machinery. He believed that the industrial system was an extension of the logic of the human mind – rational systems would lead to the best results.

Unfortunately for Henry Ford, many of his assembly line workers did not share his enthusiasm for repetitive physical labour of the kind offered at his Detroit factory. Working for Ford not only meant repetition, it meant committing yourself to a system of harsh discipline while at work and to a lifestyle outside of the factory gates 'free from any malicious practice derogatory to good physical manhood and moral character'. Ford was opposed to gambling, drinking alcohol, smoking and sex outside marriage. He set up a sociological department to monitor the behaviour of his employees.

As the company became more successful, Ford became more and more exacting, insisting that the organisation run according to the systems he created. Today, he might be described as being a 'control freak'. He appointed people to be his immediate subordinates who were authoritarian; for example Charles Sorensen became his Factory Superintendent.

Among line managers, office workers and shop personnel Charles Sorenson quickly became the most feared man in the organisation. On the shopfloor he was known as 'Iron Charlie', master of the speed up. In 1921 on Ford's orders he ruthlessly doubled the speed of the assembly line, while at the same time cutting the number of production workers by 30 per cent and cutting wages by 25 per cent.

Managers were also subject to ruthless control. Managers who questioned Ford's authority were sometimes forced to resign or fired. At the height of the purges of management, the sociological department was abolished and replaced by the more ruthless service department. Ford controlled by fear. He believed that humanitarian and social considerations had no place in the work environment. Within his own organisation Ford regarded any sign of humanitarianism with contempt. 'There is altogether too much reliance on good feeling in our business organisation.'

movements made by production line workers in order to reduce the movements and tasks performed to the minimum for maximum efficiency.

Labour tasks were thus reduced to machine-like efficiency. He felt that operatives would be prepared to work in this way to gain more pay.

Taylor saw the purpose of scientific management as being to find the single best way of organising work. He outlined four principles of scientific management:

1. The development of a science of work to replace old 'rule-of-thumb' methods. If workers met work goals they would be rewarded by higher pay.
2. The scientific selection and development of workers, so that they would be trained to be 'first class' at their tasks.
3. Bringing together the science of work and scientifically trained workers to produce the best results.
4. The scientific division of work between managers and workers so that they were all working towards the highest goals.

Modern derivatives of Fordism and scientific management

The modern reader may find the doctrines of Taylor and Ford frightening in their regimentation of people. However, it is important to recognise that elements of Taylorism and Fordism are still with us. Mass production factories continue to give priority to the production system dominated by machinery rather than to the needs of the employee. Also, Fordist techniques are employed in many businesses which predominantly employ part-time, and unskilled labour. Henry Ford boasted that he could take a boy straight off an American farm to work in one of his factories because the work was so simple, and controlled by machinery. Today, Fordist machines and systems dominate work in fast food outlets and at supermarket checkouts. In the fast food outlet the machinery tells the operative what to do. A buzzer goes when toast needs to be turned over, or when a burger has cooked. The parts of the burger are assembled in a pre-determined way, etc. At the supermarket checkout the operative follows a series of Fordist instructions – 'print the cheque', 'check the customer's signature', 'give the customer the receipt', etc.

Human relations approaches
Elton Mayo's Hawthorne experiments
The scientific management approach can be contrasted with the human relations school of thought. Elton Mayo and a team of

researchers from the Harvard Business School carried out a series of experiments from 1927 to 1932 at the Hawthorne plant of Western Electric Company in Chicago. Initially Mayo had taken on board some of the assumptions of the scientific managers, believing that physical conditions in the working environment, the aptitudes of workers and financial incentives were the key ingredients in motivation.

With this in mind, Mayo had experimented with different levels of heating, lighting, lengths and frequencies of rest periods and other variables. However, the results of the experiments were inconclusive; for example, Mayo and his team were surprised to find that wide variations in the level of lighting had little or no effect on output.

During the course of the experiments, Mayo found that the productivity of the group studied kept climbing, irrespective of various changes. Mayo came to the conclusion that, as a result of the experiment, a great deal of attention had been given to the group and members of the group had come to feel much closer ties with each other. Mayo felt that this was the important factor, and his work led to an appreciation of the importance of the **informal group** in industry (i.e. the formation of bonds within groups of workers).

Motivation and teamwork

The Hawthorne studies moved the emphasis from the individual worker to the worker as a member of a social group. Mayo suggested that managers should establish and maintain a sense of group purpose in industry. In recent years there has been a widespread development of teamwork approaches in industry which clearly follow on from this earlier work.

Following on from the development of human relations approaches to management a number of key thinkers have made major contributions to thinking about people management. In particular much has been written about ways of creating genuine **motivation** in the workforce.

Herzberg

Frederick Herzberg (*The Motivation to Work*, 1959) has shown managers rewarding workers for efforts as suggested by the scientific management approach rarely works in practice. Herzberg showed that you can move people by a range of rewards and punishments which he termed positive and negative **KITA** ('kicks in the ass'). However, **movement** is different from motivation.

Herzberg argues that the problem with moving people is short term and usually stops once the force is removed. Outside force only generates movement.

In contrast motivation is a drive that comes from within an individual, and is a function of individual will. People do things because the outcome is appealing to them. Motivation is goal-directed behaviour.

The implication for the human resource manager is that you need to find out about what drives individuals, and thus motivates them. Herzberg felt that true motivation stems from providing **satisfiers** in work such as making jobs more interesting or giving employees more responsibility.

Maslow

Abraham Maslow (*Motivation and Personality*, 1954) was one of the first writers to describe motivation in terms of human needs, and these ideas have often been applied in the workplace. Maslow identified a **hierarchy of needs** at eight levels (Figure 2). The first four of these needs are fundamental goals which need to be met. The top four can be pursued in any order depending on a person's wants or circumstances (once the bottom four have been met).

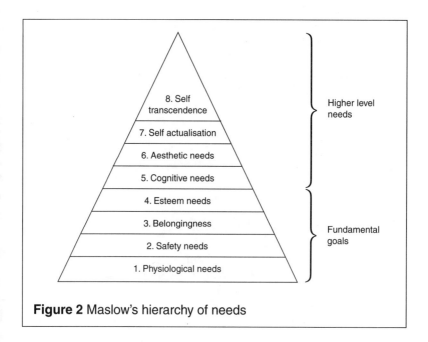

Figure 2 Maslow's hierarchy of needs

Physiological needs are for the basic needs of food, shelter, and clothing which can be bought with a reasonable living wage from work. **Safety** needs can be met in a safe working environment in which individual employees are not threatened, intimidated or made to work in dangerous conditions. **Belongingness** can be created in the work environment from working in a team. **Esteem** can be created by giving a person a valued job role or position. These four needs should be provided in the modern business organisation. The other needs are also important – such as the need for intellectual stimulation (**cognitive needs**), or for beauty (**aesthetic needs**), while **self actualisation** is concerned with personal fulfilment, and **self transcendence** is concerned with exceeding personal expectations.

Maslow suggested that only 1 per cent of the population ever self actualise. Critical to Maslow's ideas was that no one stays at one level for a long time. We constantly try to move up to higher levels while forces outside our control try to push us down. It seems that while personally we push to achieve our higher level needs, fate and circumstance work against us.

Maslow's notion of a hierarchy of needs provides managers with useful insights into people management. The manager needs to find out where individuals are located in terms of Maslow's hierarchy in order to identify suitable motivational factors. However, more importantly the manager should seek to provide individual employees with the skills and knowledge which will enable them to push up the hierarchical ladder permanently.

Conclusions of human relations approaches
Herzberg, Maslow and other researchers have provided human resource managers with useful insights into motivation, in particular that:

- people are motivated by unmet goals which drive them to achieve
- drivers are far more complex than simple material rewards
- the most powerful drivers seem to be intrinsic rather than extrinsic.

Empowerment-based HRM approaches
Is supervision always necessary?
The work of Elton Mayo and the Human Relations School criticised Taylorism and suggested that involving workers had strong business as well as moral benefits. Workers could be self-motivated and carry out good work without close supervision.

Development of empowerment strategies

In the 1960s the idea of **job enrichment** (giving employees increased responsibility/and or recognition) became popular as a means of providing meaningful work for employees, placing more emphasis on intrinsic motivation, for example by providing some decision making opportunities.

In the 1970s there was greater interest in industrial democracy which emphasised workers' rights to participate. Government support for greater **worker participation** was widespread in Western Europe in the 1970s apart from the United Kingdom (during the Thatcher era).

By the 1980s new forms of participation were developed which emphasised **employee involvement**, for example in quality circles, team briefing and profit sharing initiatives. These 1980s' developments of the empowerment theme were very much management led.

The prevailing message given by the literature of empowerment was that management should give more decision making powers to employees in order to unleash their entrepreneurial skills and to make the organisations more responsive to their markets and hence more competitive.

Tom Peters

Peters and Waterman's 1982 book *In Search of Excellence* was very influential (as popular versions of their ideas were widely publicised in the business press) in creating a new business wisdom which was widely adopted including slogans such as 'Productivity through People' and 'Autonomy and Entrepreneurship'. Empowerment, it was suggested, involved managers unleashing the talents of individuals by dismantling organisational bureaucracy. Managers were exhorted to trust and involve employees by giving individual employees greater discretion with regards to how they carried out their jobs.

By 1995, Tom Peters in another popular management text, *The Pursuit of Wow!*, was arguing that:

> '*Hierarchies are going, going, gone. The average Mike or Mary is being asked to take on extraordinary responsibility. He or she may be on the payroll or, at least as likely, an independent contractor. In any event, the hyperfast moving, wired-up, re-engineered, quality-obsessed organisation – virtual or not – will succeed or fail on the strength of the trust that the remaining tiny cadre of managers places in the folks working on the front line.*'

In terms of people management, employers were urged to move away from an approach based on compliance, hierarchical authority and limited employee discretion to one where there was greater emphasis on high trust relations, teamworking and empowerment, with calls for employee commitment and the utilisation of workforce expertise.

At the same time the Total Quality Management (TQM) movement that infiltrated from Japan encouraged **continuous improvement** by those involved in a process and this introduced elements of bottom-up issue identification and problem solving. The wider use of TQM helped to empower employees by delegating functions that were previously the preserve of more senior organisational members leading to the creation of participation on a permanent basis.

The struggle to establish empowerment

While many senior managers were committed to empowerment because of its motivational potential and because of its humanising influence on the work place, it was not always easy to convince the workforce that empowerment was in 'their interest'. This was because during the 1980s and 1990s aspects of the business environment required businesses to cut back on costs – particularly labour costs. As a result there was also a profoundly negative force which drove many of the empowerment initiatives of the time. In the 1980s and 1990s rationalisation and downsizing were very much the order of the day. In this context empowerment became a business necessity as the destaffed and delayered organisation could no longer function as before. In this set of circumstances, empowerment was inevitable as tasks had to be allocated to the survivors in the new organisation.

The problems of HRM
Hard or soft HRM?

HRM has been criticised by some because it is based on a **unitary view** of the organisation, i.e. it is based on the assumption that everyone in the organisation agrees to pull in a common direction and that they have shared interests. In particular, HRM is criticised for the assumption that this unitary perspective is the management perspective. In contrast, other thinkers see social organisations as being based on a **plurality** of interests, for example shareholder interests, manager interests, employee interests, etc. Pluralists would argue that empowerment only involves the transfer of powers that managers are willing to divest to further the interests of the organisation.

While the idea of Human Resource Management has been widely welcomed in management circles, there is considerable debate over how well HRM has been applied in organisations in the UK. While many managers pay lip service to soft HRM many would argue that what actually materialises is hard HRM in which people-based initiatives are primarily driven by the interests of the organisation rather than being a genuine two-way process. Indeed some writers have argued that in any case 'soft is hard', i.e. just another way of winning employee compliance. Clark and Salaman (1998) suggest that many employees have little faith in new management ideas because they don't see them as lasting. They are highly critical of management's ability to persist on a single course for more than a short while. Workers are reluctant to respond with enthusiasm to management initiatives because they feel that they will soon be replaced by 'the next best idea'.

Is HRM effective?

In spite of the criticisms levelled above, there is a lot of case study evidence and useful quantitative evidence to support the view that employees do respond favourably to **'bundles' of Human Resource Management initiatives** and that the greater number of initiatives adopted by organisations, the more motivated and satisfied are the employees in their place of work.

Each year the Institute of Personnel and Development (IPD) carries out a survey of employment relations in the UK. The survey covers a stratified random sample of 1000 workers (and is confined to organisations employing 10 people or more). The sample is stratified to ensure representative quotas of the working population with respect to age and gender (it inevitably excludes those who are not in work). The data are collected by telephone interviews conducted by the Harris organisation. Some of the results of the 1997 survey are shown in Table 1.

By using these twelve aspects as being representative of HRM practice the researchers then went on to look at the relationship between the number of HRM initiatives and satisfaction and well-being (Tables 2 and 3).

Table 1 Workers' reports on the presence of HRM practices

	Percentage		
	Yes	No	Don't know
Employer provides you with reasonable opportunities to express grievances and raise personal concerns	86	13	1
Employer provides you with sufficient opportunities for training and development	84	16	0
Organisation keeps you informed about business issues and how well it is doing	80	18	1
Policy of single status	72	24	4
Employer has effective systems for dealing with bullying and harassment at work	62	22	17
Serious attempt to make jobs of people like you as interesting and variable as possible	58	38	3
When new positions come up in management, the company normally tries to fill them with people from inside the organisation rather then recruiting them from outside (percentage who try to fill from within)	57	37	6
Workplace has programme for employee involvement in decision making such as self-directed work teams, Total Quality Management or Quality Circles	45	51	4
Stated policy of deliberately avoiding compulsory redundancies and lay-offs	44	33	22
Your organisation tries to relate your pay to your performance in some way	41	58	1
Some sort of profit sharing or share ownership scheme through which people like you get rewarded if the business is doing well	36	62	2
Have taken part in a staff attitude survey carried out by current employer in the last two years	33	67	0

Source: Harris organisation, 1997

Table 2 HRM practices and employees' satisfaction and well-being

		\multicolumn{5}{c}{Number of HR practices}				
		0–3	4–6	7–9	10–12	All
		\multicolumn{5}{c}{Percentage}				
How secure do you feel in your present job?	Very secure	20	33	40	46	37
	Fairly secure	52	51	50	43	49
	Fairly insecure	14	11	8	9	10
	Very insecure	13	4	3	2	4
How often do you feel under excessive pressure at work?	All the time	19	5	10	9	9
	Quite often	32	38	40	44	39
	Every now and then	32	38	37	39	37
	Rarely	12	11	9	6	9
	Never	5	7	4	2	5
Overall, which of the following statements best describes how satisfied you have felt with your job over the past few weeks?	Couldn't be more satisfied	4	6	10	12	9
	Very satisfied	10	28	32	35	29
	Quite satisfied	37	41	40	41	40
	Just about satisfied	27	17	14	11	16
	Not at all satisfied	21	7	4	2	6
	n =	100	308	413	179	1000

Source: Harris organisation, 1997

Table 3 HRM practices and motivation

		|				
		Number of HR practices				
		0–3	4–6	7–9	10–12	All
		Percentage				
How motivated	Very motivated	17	29	38	45	35
do you feel in your	Fairly motivated	48	49	49	47	48
present job?	Not very motivated	16	17	10	7	13
	Not at all motivated	18	4	3	1	4
When you get up	All the time	11	13	12	13	12
in the morning,	Most of the time	20	34	55	55	45
how often do you	Sometimes	30	32	20	21	25
really look forward	Rarely	19	12	6	6	9
to going to work?	Never	19	9	7	4	8
	n =	100	308	413	179	1000

Source: Harris organisation, 1997

The information provided in the tables tends to suggest that where more progressive HR practices are in place, workers report more positive outcomes. This appears to support the adoption of Human Resource Management, and in particular, for a number of practices in combination rather than specific practices in isolation.

KEY WORDS

Fordism	Hierarchy of needs
Scientific management	Self actualisation
Human relations	Job enrichment
Empowerment	Worker participation
Time and motion studies	Employee involvement
Informal group	Continuous improvement
Motivation	Unitary view
KITA	Plurality
Movement	'Bundles' of Human Resource
Satisfiers	Management initiatives

Further reading

Dransfield, R. *et al*., Chapter 19 in *Human Resource Management for Higher Awards*, Heinemann, 1996.

Kennedy, C., Chapters 9, 15, 26, 27, 31 and 39 in *Guide to the Management Gurus*, Century Business, 1998.

Peters, T., Chapters 8 and 9 in *The Tom Peters Seminar: Crazy Times Call for Crazy Organisations*, Macmillan, 1995.

Schermerhorn, J.R. *et al*., Chapter 6 in *Managing Organisational Behaviour*, John Wiley, 1998.

Further references

Herzberg, F., *The Motivation to Work*. John Wiley and Sons, 1959.

Maslow, A., *Motivation and Personality*. Harper 1954.

Peters, T., *The Pursuit of Wow!*. Macmillan, 1995.

Kohn, A., 'Punished by Rewards: The trouble with gold starts, incentive plans, and praise and other bribes'. Houghton Mifflin, 1997.

Taylor, F.W., *The Principles of Scientific Management*. Harper, 1911.

Clark, T. and Salaman, G., 'Telling Tales: Management Gurus'. Narratives and the construction of managerial identity'. *Journal of Management Studies*, Vol. 32, no. 2, 137–161, 1998.

West, D., 'Human Resource Management – The Workers's Verdict'. *Human Resource Management Journal*, Vol. 9, No. 3, 1999.

Useful website

Personnel Review, a journal with detailed topics about managing people and personnel related topics: www.hrhq.com/

Essay topics

1. 'People are an organisation's most important resource.' Discuss. [25 marks]
2. 'Scientific management is not dead. It can be found everywhere in modern British industry.' Discuss this statement. [25 marks]

Data response question

Family friendly employment policies are defined by the government's Women's Unit as those which help women and men to balance the demands of paid work and family life.

A survey carried out by the journal *Labour Research* into the practices of a number of major UK companies revealed the results shown in Table A. The survey covered a range of aspects of working arrangements – namely part-time working, flexi-hours, voluntary reduced hours (or 'V-time'), job-sharing and term-time only working.

Table A Family friendly policies of some of the largest UK companies

Company	No. of UK-based employees	% Women	% Part time	Parental leave	Time off for domestic incidents	Flexi-hours	V-time	Job sharing	Working from home	Term-time only
Tesco	172 000	67	30	c	d	d	d	d	no	d
British Telecom	120 000	26	nk	no	d	d	d	yes	yes	no
Boots	80 000	73	60	c	yes	d	d	d	d	d
ASDA	80 000	75	80	c	d	no	yes	d	no	yes
Lloyds TSB	77 000	68	nk	yes	d	yes	yes	yes	yes	yes
Safeway	74 000	59	66	no	yes	yes	d	d	d	d
NatWest	70 000	60	18	c	d	d	d	d	d	d
Bass	65 000	50	50	d	d	d	no	d	d	no
HSBC	48 000	63	23	no	d	d	no	d	d	d

c = career breaks d = on discretionary bases, nk = not known.

Source: Labour Research, July 1999

1. (a) Which of the organisations shown in Table A had the highest percentages of women and part-timers? [3 marks]
   (b) Explain why there are more women and part-timers working for these firms. [3 marks]
2. Does Table A indicate that large employers in this country are employing family friendly policies or not? [6 marks]
3. How might large companies benefit from utilising family friendly policies? [4 marks]
4. Explain how one of the family friendly policies examined in the survey would increase labour flexibility, and show how this would benefit (a) the employer, and (b) the employing organisation. [9 marks]

Chapter Three

The changing context of Human Resource Management

'Flexibility, the capacity to produce a range of different products at the lowest total cost, is increasingly seen as more important than reducing the cost of any one product to the technically attainable minimum.'
Ken Starkey and Alan McKinlay

In the early twenty-first century, people and human intelligence have been able, at least in some situations, to reclaim their rightful place as the dominant wealth creating factors in society. This role had been usurped by physical capital – buildings and machinery – during the Industrial Age which saw some of the most destructive (yet highly productive) forces set loose on human relationships – not least of which was the creation of Industrial Systems. Of course, the remnants of the Industrial Age associated with Fordism are still with us but the influence of top-down mechanistic hierarchies and systems are less prevalent.

The move to flexibility

Fordism was successful in a world in which large numbers of customers had identical wants which could be serviced by a rational, product-specific manufacturing procedure. The Model-T Ford was the perfect example of this. While millions of customers were looking for a cheap and effective family vehicle – the Model-T met their need. They could 'have any colour they liked as long as it was black', and millions of such cars ran off Ford's assembly line.

For many years, **Fordist marketing and production strategies** were based on product market stability and the maximisation of large-scale economies (the range of benefits of producing products on a large rather than a small scale) through a highly integrated division of labour based on dedicated machinery, the deskilling of labour and direct managerial control. Tasks were set out in fine detail and work was planned centrally.

All of this was to change in the post-1980s world. After the 1980s Western manufacturers were woken up with a jolt to find increasing competition, first from Japan, and later from the South-East Asian

Tiger economies. During the 1980s the 'sunrise' countries began to concentrate on sophisticated products – cars, cameras and electronic goods of all kinds. They also turned their dedication and dynamism into services – banking and home entertainment among them.

Their success was based partly on the very competitive prices they were able to ask for their products and services, but mainly on their quality. That took the West by surprise.

The concept of 'total quality management', developed in the US after the end of the Second World War in 1945, but implemented at first only in Japan, changed the balance of world trade and caused every company in the West to rethink its attitudes, policies and above all its structure. Total quality management can only operate when responsibility and power are delegated downwards. Hierarchies cannot sustain the effort required – the buck can be passed far too easily. Company size became less important than employee motivation, which is easier to achieve in small groups (or small companies).

In the new competitive world order the key strategic task facing the organisation became responsiveness to new forms of fast changing demand and the key organisation task: the efficient and innovative management of a portfolio of associated rather than standardised products.

These demands place a premium upon increased work organisation **flexibility**, and the active co-operation of an upskilled more versatile workforce. As demand becomes less stable, more differentiated and more **dynamic** (fast changing) it becomes important to build into an organisation the capacity for flexibility of response.

Flexible working

During the 1980s the UK economy developed levels of flexibility well in excess of those in competing nations in Western Europe, and throughout the 1990s and early 2000s both Conservative and Labour governments have set out to encourage flexible labour markets. There are a number of aspects of **flexible working practice**, for example:

- **Functional flexibility** refers to the ability of employees to perform a number of different tasks often as a result of training for multi-skilling.
- **Numerical flexibility** refers to the ability of firms to adjust the number of workers or the number of hours worked in line with changes in the level of demand for their goods and services. Typically this refers to the use of part-time, temporary and sub-contracted workers. A good example of this is the way in which

large supermarket chains commonly vary the number of hours they allocate to employees in the following week depending on the profit figures in the previous week. A number of firms have moved their employees on to annual hours contracts, whereby instead of employing someone for say 35 hours per week throughout the year, the employer estimates the number of hours it requires an employee throughout the year and then creates a contract setting out this annual requirement. This gives the firm the flexibility to use the employees' services when they are required (and not to use them when they are not required).

- **Temporal, or working time, flexibility** can be seen as a particular form of numerical flexibility, relating to changes in the number and timing of hours worked from day to day or week to week, for example through flexi-time or annual hours contracts.
- The use of more temporary and contract workers and other methods of flexible working has changed Britain's employment patterns. These changes stemmed from the need to increase productivity, flexibility and cost control. Other examples of flexible arrangements include the development of job shares and 'hot desking' (where as one employee leaves their desk to go home, another employee slips into their workstation).
- **Locational flexibility** in terms of place of work, has seen the widespread development of **homeworking,** so that the employee can work from home (often using Information and Communications Technology) rather than working directly on the organisation's premises.

During the 1990s the vast majority of the UK's largest organisations were restructured, leading to job losses at all levels.

The flexible firm
A business concept that grew in popularity in the last decade of the twentieth century was that of the 'flexible firm'.

Up until the 1980s most large organisations had a large core of full-time workers who expected a job for life. Throughout the country, employees would start working with an employer like Boots or Raleigh after leaving school. Brothers, sisters, parents, grandparents, uncles and aunts might all work for the same employer.

Today, the pool of **core workers** in an organisation has been severely slimmed down. Instead, organisations rely more and more on peripheral and external workers to carry out work tasks (Figure 3).

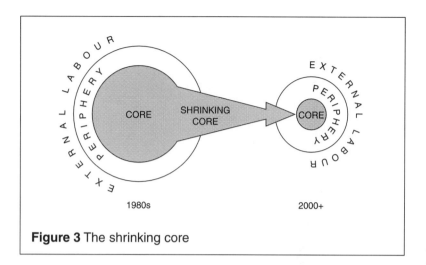

Figure 3 The shrinking core

Core workers tend to be multi-skilled, full time, enjoying good pay conditions and benefits (although on the downside core workers tend to work the longest hours, often in stressful work situations).

Peripheral workers are short term, temporary, part time and receiving less favourable pay, conditions and benefits.

External workers are those who are not employees of the firm (agency temps, workers in contracted-out services and the self-employed).

The flexible firm sets out to cut its labour costs to a minimum by limiting core workers, relative to peripheral and external workers.

The spread of the flexible firm presents considerable challenges to the people manager because peripheral and external workers' primary allegiance is not to the organisation, while core workers may see that the security of their position has been eroded, while they are expected to work longer hours in more demanding conditions.

The psychological contract

In an increasingly insecure world of work writers about human resources have increasingly come to stress the importance of the **psychological contract** that is forged between the employee and the organisation. While a contract of employment sets out the legal relationship between the two parties it does not forge a 'personal relationship'. In the twenty-first century Western society emphasises 'individualistic' values which translate in the workplace into the

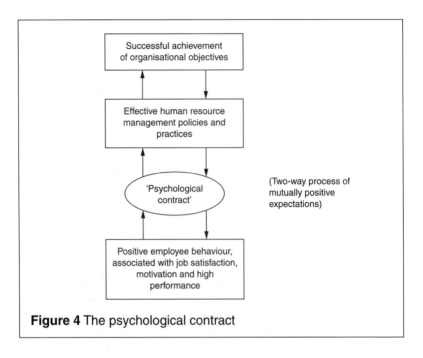

Figure 4 The psychological contract

individuals' relations with their employer. The set of expectations on both sides has been termed a 'psychological contract' (Figure 4).

From the management perspective the significance of the psychological contract lies in the impact it can have on employee behaviour, job satisfaction, motivation and performance, and hence on the ability of the organisation to meet its objectives.

Typically definitions of the psychological contract are based on people's perceptions and include aspects such as loyalty, trust and recognition. Mutual obligations lie at the heart of this contact, and consist of beliefs held by the two sides to the contract, that the other party has made a promise to act in a supportive, caring and helpful way in terms of creating mutually favourable and positive working relationships.

The rise of the new economy

In the early 1990s unemployment in the European Union stood at 20 million and many commentators were gloomy about the ability of the economy to create anything like full employment. The fear was that competition from South-East Asia and the widespread growth of Information and Communications Technologies (ICT) would permanently wipe out many jobs in the West.

While unemployment at the start of the new millennium is still unacceptably high, there is an increased optimism about the job market. For example, a Treasury analysis of regional patterns of unemployment in the UK published in February 2000 noted that the number of unemployed people per job vacancy was lower than at any point since 1975. The report also indicated that where pockets of unemployment are particularly high there is usually work to be found within a few miles of these pockets, leading the government to seek new ways of encouraging mobility in the unemployed.

The development of the networked economy in the United States

A group of economists (based largely in the United States) have come to identify the potential of what they term the 'new economy' to transform output and employment on a global scale in a generally favourable direction. In particular they focus on the ability of new technologies and innovations to create a dynamic economy which brings with it a host of new opportunities and with it new jobs.

The 1990s saw a continual rise in the national income of the United States at around 3 per cent driven forward by the leverage effect of the impact of Information and Communications Technology in industry. Kevin Kelly (1998) argues that the new economy is increasingly based on the logic of **networks**. He believes that the combination of two innovations – the silicon chip and the silicate glass fibre have unleashed the power of the pervasive net which is creating a global network society.

The network effect

Kelly (1998) describes the impact of the network effect in the following way:

'Take 4 acquaintances; there are 12 distinct one-to-one friendships among them. If we add a fifth friend to the group, the friendship network increases to 20 different relations; 6 friends makes 30 connections; 7 makes 42. As the number of members goes beyond 10, the total number of relationships among the friends escalates rapidly, when the number of people (n) involved is large, the total number of connections can be approximated as simply $n \times n$ or n^2. Thus a thousand members can have a million friendships.'

The economist Brian Arthur (1994) uses the term 'increasing returns' in the context of the network economy to describe a situation in which as the number of connections between people and things add up, the consequences of those connections multiply out even faster, so that initial successes aren't self-limiting but self-feeding.

Traditional industrial economies of scale increased value gradually and linearly – small efforts yielded small results, while large efforts gave large results. Networks, on the other hand, increase value exponentially – small efforts reinforce one another so that results can quickly snowball into an avalanche. The other key difference between the new and the old is that while before industrial economies of scale stemmed from the efforts of a single organisation to outpace the competition, in contrast, network increasing returns are created and shared by the entire network.

The dramatic impact of the Internet

The best example of networking is the development of the Internet. Use of the Internet is growing literally exponentially. The Internet has made it possible for vast quantities of ideas to be shared to the mutual benefit of organisations and researchers from across the globe.

The real benefits of the networked economy will increasingly become evident further into the new century. There are lags between technical developments and any economic impact they might have, because businesses have to adopt the new technology and invest a lot in it. Even in the US, rapid investment in ICT software and hardware dates back only to the start of 1992.

The US economic historian Paul David described how it took 40 years for US industry to reorganise in order to exploit efficiently the electric dynamo. On top of the amount of investment, it demanded other social and legal pre-conditions, such as limited liability, development of the banking system, and free trade. But when all that was in place, the result was staggering: mass production and mass consumption.

The impact of the Internet is much more rapid. While it took radio 37 years to reach a global audience of 50 million, and television 15 years, it took the world wide web just three years after the development of the web browser in 1994. On the deficit side a major impact of the networked economy has been to create greater uncertainty and change in organisational life than ever before. Organisations and their people have had to become more flexible, putting an increasing strain on the psychological contract between employer and employee.

Charles Handy (1994) has argued that as security of employment

Staff get in on lucrative dot.com act

LISA BUCKINGHAM

CGU, one of the UK's biggest insurers, has become one of a handful of companies which is attempting to tackle competition from Internet rivals by encouraging its own staff to propose dot.com ventures.

The company sees its support for staff Internet projects not only as a way to expand its own business and keep a finger in new insurance developments but also as a way to retain employees who might otherwise simply decamp, taking their ideas and their experience with them.

Traditional businesses are increasingly recognising that they risk losing their most entrepreneurial employees unless they can devise outlets for their cutting edge ventures as well as the potentially lucrative rewards which are now associated with so many Internet start ups.

CGU says about 50 projects have so far been given the green light and the first off the ground is bluecycle.com, a cyber auction site selling stolen goods recovered by the police and other insurance salvage goods. A homebuying site, which is likely to offer mortgages and insurance, is forecast to kick off in the spring.

The cyber-cultivation scheme is known as Siliconwharf, reflecting its base in a warehouse alongside the River Thames.

Guardian, 21 February 2000

with a single employer decreases then individuals will need to increasingly build their own identities and careers rather than subordinating their needs to the organisation, while at the same time organisations should increasingly help their workers to maintain employability through ongoing training and development programmes.

Flexible labour markets lead to success

A number of American economists believe that the comparative flexibility of US labour markets compared to European ones helps to explain the relative success of the two areas in creating employment in recent years. Supporters of the new economy believe it is inevitable that many new jobs will quickly disappear again.

Donald Hicks of the University of Texas studied the life span of Texan businesses between the 1970s and early 1990s and found that this span had reduced by half. However, areas which had the shortest business life spans also often had the fastest growing numbers of new jobs and the highest wages. 'Rather than considering jobs as a fixed sum to be protected and increased,' Hicks argued, the government should encourage economic churning – on continually recycling redundant labour from one job to another. Hicks contrasted the European Union where between 1980 and 1995 12 million government jobs were protected by the state, resulting in inflexibility leading to 5 million jobs being lost in the private sector. In contrast, during the same period in the flexible US labour markets 44 million old jobs were lost from the private sector, while 73 million new jobs were generated in the private sector, and 12 million jobs were maintained in the government sector. The 'new economists' believe that it is through flexibility that organisations and individuals will be best able to reinvent themselves in order to secure continuing employability and business success in the modern turbulent world.

The 'intelligent organisation' and the 'intelligent worker'

In post-industrial Britain service industries now account for the majority of employment opportunities, and the current strength of the British economy rests upon flexible working practices employed within service and knowledge-based industries, e.g. hospitality, leisure and tourism, media and communications, and science and technology. For example, computer software, music, fashion, design, film, broadcasting, publishing and the performing arts are sectors of creativity which in 1999 accounted for some £50 billion of economic activity and more than a million jobs (interestingly the term 'knowledge worker' entered the Oxford dictionary in 1999).

Intelligent organisations are ones whose strength (including the strength of their balance sheets) rests in intellectual capital rather than physical capital. In the Industrial Age machinery, plant and other items of physical capital drove the industrial process.

Today, it is the brainpower of knowledge workers that is at the forefront. It is brainpower that enables an organisation to identify customer needs and requirements; it is brainpower that enables an organisation to engage in product research and development; it is brainpower that enables the organisation to produce the best Information and Communications Technology solutions to problems; and it is brainpower that enables the organisation to come up with the most appropriate promotional activities.

Microsoft takes pole position

In 1998 the transformation in industry and society to the domination of the knowledge organisation was symbolised by the arrival of Microsoft as the most valuable company in the United States. On 13 September 1998 Microsoft toppled General Electric as the highest valued company. GE is still overwhelmingly an industrial manufacturer providing big ticket (high priced) items such as large domestic appliances from washing machines to cookers as well as aircraft engines. The company continues to be successful but not as successful as Microsoft.

While GE represents the Industrial Age, Microsoft represents the Information Age with its dominating presence in providing software systems to personal computers and its success in exploiting the explosion of the Internet. Microsoft is a company which is very much based on the knowledge and expertise of its employees. The generosity of the company in distributing shares to employees has created no fewer than 4000 millionaires around its Redmond, Washington base – the so-called Microsoft Millionnaires.

Competitive advantage through human resources

Intelligent organisations like Microsoft recognise that knowledge workers need to be valued because they add the most value to products. Organisations gain **competitive advantage** (i.e. a distinct edge over rival organisations in the eyes of consumers) by being able to offer more desirable benefits. These benefits are created through the process of adding value to the final product or service. In the intelligent organisation these benefits are created through the brainpower and creative intelligence of knowledge workers. In recent years there have been striking examples of the ways in which knowledge workers create value to all sorts of organisations, not just through creating new products such as better treatments for AIDS and cancer but in every stage of value addition. For example, the small group of creatives who came up with the Levis in the laundrette advertisement added millions of dollars to the value of the brand, and the group of researchers working for Mars that developed the Mars ice cream created a new product concept that has not only led to millions of pounds of extra profits for Mars, but also for rival producers of confectionery and sweet-based ice creams.

The intelligent organisation seeks to hang on to its intelligent people because they are worth it. And, of course it is a two-way process. Knowledge workers also realise that they can use their knowledge to best effect by working with or for dynamic asset rich companies which are able to provide the knowledge worker with the means to add value to knowledge (e.g. through links and connections, through marketing expertise, through access to scarce, and expensive resources, etc.).

The intelligent organisation must therefore place a key strategic emphasis on human resource policies in order to win the commitment of its people. The intelligent organisation therefore has to give a high priority to building effective psychological contracts, for example by offering excellent training and personal development opportunities.

KEY WORDS

Fordist marketing and
    production strategies
Flexibility
Dynamic (demand)
Flexible working practice
Numerical flexibility
Temporal (working time)
    flexibility
Hot desking
Homeworking
Flexible firm

Core workers
Peripheral workers
External workers
Psychological contract
New economy
Networks
Increasing returns
Knowledge worker
Intelligent organisations
Competitive advantage

Further reading

Dransfield, R. *et al.*, Chapter 1 in *Human Resource Management for Higher Awards*, Heinemann, 1996.

Foot, M. and Hook, C., Chapter 6 in *Introducing Human Resource Management*, Longman, 1999.

Handy, C., Chapters 1–6 in *The Empty Raincoat, Making Sense of the Future*, Hutchinson, 1994.

Kelly, K., Chapters 1–6 in *New Rules for the New Economy*, Fourth Estate, 1998.

Further references

Arthur, W.B., *Increasing Returns and Path Dependence in the Economy*. University of Michigan Press, 1994.

Dransfield, D.L.S., 'Is the new economy the way forward?' *General Studies Review*. April 2000.

Starkey, K. and McKinlay, A., *Strategy and the Human Resource – Ford and the Search for Competitive Advantage*. Blackwell, 1993.

Useful website

The most complete web site for the new economy, including links to other web sites on the information and network economy: www.sims.berkeley.edu/resources/infoecon/

Essay topics

1. (a) Why have firms increasingly adopted the flexible firm model? [9 marks]
   (b) What are the drawbacks of adopting this model:
     (i) for employees in the organisation? [7 marks]
     (ii) for the organisation itself? [7 marks]
2. (a) How can firms achieve flexibility? [10 marks]
   (b) Contrast and evaluate the relative merits of two examples of flexible working practice which are currently popular in UK business organisations. [15 marks]

Data response question

Bank staff anxiety as Barclays launches new remote banking service

UNiFI, the finance union representing more than two-thirds of all Barclays Bank staff, today gave a mixed reception to the announcement by the Bank of the creation of a new telephone banking centre in Sunderland on Wearside, albeit bringing with it 2000 new jobs to the area.

The union's concern focuses on the question of full union recognition rights since UNiFI has experienced a two-year battle with Barclaycall at its existing sites in Coventry and Salford Quays (Manchester) to establish such rights for employees in the Bank's telephone banking services. Despite recent polls at Barclaycall, which indicated the most popular option is union representation, Barclaycall has refused to accept UNiFI as the recognised representative of staff.

Disadvantageous terms
This issue is of particularly pressing concern as pay and terms for staff at Barclaycall are considerably worse than those for the majority of employees in Barclays plc. The move towards telephone banking and remote centralisation due to 'clustering' of branches

can often mean that those who lose their jobs in other parts of the Bank could be forced to take a pay cut to remain in employment. UNiFI does not believe this is acceptable.

Depletion of branch network affects customer service
Additionally, UNiFI is concerned that existing jobs in bank service centres which take phone calls from customers to their branches may be threatened by the extension of the newly launched service. The union believes this move indicates yet another threat to the branch banking network which has traditionally had such a prominent place in the nation's high streets.

Threat to current jobs
Sarah Messenger, UNiFI National Officer, comments, 'UNiFI always welcomes the creation of jobs and the North East is an area where the union has been pressing for a new centre to be located. However, the fact that the union is not recognised in this centre is a matter of major concern for staff that currently work at Barclaycall and for those who may be looking to work in Barclays in the future. It is hoped that this new project will not remove jobs from existing staff.'

Source: press release from UNiFI, the financial services trade union, 26 February 1998

1. Why did UNiFI have mixed feelings about the creation of the new telephone banking centre in Sunderland? [3 marks]
2. To what extent might the new development be seen as cutting across the notion of a psychological contract between employees and their employer? [6 marks]
3. What does the case indicate is happening to the core workforce of Barclays (and other banks)? [5 marks]
4. Why is Barclays making this change? [4 marks]
5. What are the implications of changes like the one described in the case for the development of Human Resource Management in the UK? [7 marks]

Chapter Four

Human Resource Planning

'Strategic planning is not something a manager automatically picks up, no matter how successful he's been. Certain people are more adaptable to that orientation. Certain people have qualities of mind or approaches to thinking about the world that are more consistent with the kind of thinking that has to be done in planning.'
Michael. E. Porter

Introduction

This chapter starts out from the traditional view of looking at **Human Resource Planning** as involving matching an organisation's requirements for people with the availability of such people (**Manpower Planning**). The chapter then goes on to outline the nature of Human Resource Planning as part of organisation-wide strategy based on a philosophy and set of values as to how people should be treated in the workplace.

Human Resource Planning has always been a major aspect of HR work particularly in large organisations. In simple terms Human Resource Planning (what used to be called Manpower Planning) involves making sure that the organisation has available to it enough people with the appropriate skills and capabilities to meet the ongoing requirements of the organisation. In simple terms Human Resource Planning can be described as 'having the right people, in the right place, at the right time'. For example, when Nissan decided to build the new Micra car in Sunderland (place) they took on new employees (people) nine months ahead (time) of starting production in order to make sure that the right sort of training and team building (people development strategy) took place.

Human Resource Planning is therefore concerned with ensuring the **supply of labour** available to the organisation to meet ongoing **demands for labour**, and will be based on future forecasts. The demand for labour will depend on the organisation's objectives, its plans, and its expected level of economic activity. The supply of labour will come from internal sources (within the organisation, e.g. through promotions) or from external sources, e.g. through a recruitment drive (Figure 5).

Traditionally forecasting of internal supply was the centre-piece of manpower planning. It was in this area that mathematical techniques

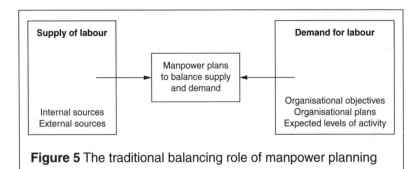

Figure 5 The traditional balancing role of manpower planning

were applied and models developed to highlight what was happening, and what would happen in the future to labour turnover (the rate at which people left jobs).

Today, this work is carried out using computer models which can be used to show the predicted flow in and out of grades of jobs in hierarchically structured organisations, i.e. manpower flow. Figure 6 shows how such a model might look with flows for promotion, wastage and recruitment of labour.

Figure 6 represents a model through which the organisation is able to calculate, for example, how it will need to meet wastage through promotion and recruitment of new employees. Of course, in the modern dynamic world of work in which organisations have moved on from hierarchies to more flexible teamwork structures, the calcu-lations have become more complex, and methods of increasing

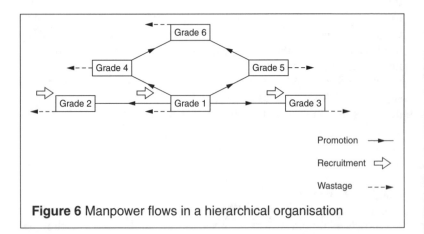

Figure 6 Manpower flows in a hierarchical organisation

supply have also changed, for example with the development of **multiskilling** (whereby an individual employee is trained to carry out many work tasks rather than just one or two). In the new world of work the manpower planners have to calculate whether existing employees will develop the skills and attitudes required for the new workplace.

Forecasting the demand for labour is the most difficult stage in Human Resource Planning. Many of the approaches used deal with lists of factors stemming from the organisation's business plan and assume a direct link with employee requirements via operating plans which contain the human resource budgets.

These lists of factors include:

- the organisation's general pattern of trading and production
- the demand for the organisation's product
- marketing plans
- changes in technology and administrative changes
- capital investment plans
- acquisitions, mergers and divestments (i.e. cutting down the scale of business operations through sales of businesses, units, etc.)
- product diversification.

The demand side of the Human Resource Plan

Demand forecasting can be carried out with a fair degree of accuracy up to one year ahead through market analysis. However, it is usually also necessary to try and piece together 2–5-year forecasts in order to plan expansion, recruitment, and 'downsizing', and training programmes.

Having established the objectives of the organisation from the corporate plan and the likely level of business activity from trading and other forecasts, the Human Resource Planner then needs to be able to translate these projections into human resource requirements based on an understanding of:

- the tasks that need to be carried out
- the skills required to complete these tasks
- how tasks can be grouped together into jobs
- numbers of employees needed to complete the estimated total work output.

Job Analysis

Job analysis is the process of gathering data about existing jobs, the activities carried out by a job holder, and the skills required to carry out a job. On an organisation-wide level job analysis should identify the full range of activities and skills that are needed by an organisation. These findings can be quantified to give a picture of current demand for labour. Job analysis of the future requirements of the organisation can then be used to forecast future demand levels. This process of forecasting future job requirements is often referred to as job modelling.

Job descriptions

Having carried out the process of job analysis, an organisation is able to create a series of **job descriptions** and **person specifications**. The job description outlines the way in which a particular job fits into the overall work structure of the organisation, including details such as the title of the job, to whom the employee is responsible, for whom the employee is responsible, and a simple description of the role and duties of the employee. A person specification goes further to highlight the mental and physical attributes required of the job holder.

Forecasting demand

There are two main ways of forecasting future demand for labour:

1. **Management estimates**. Managers may be asked to forecast their staff requirements. They will do this on the basis of past, present, and likely future requirements. Managers may base their estimates on current figures. For example, if the firms' 100 current workers can produce 1 million units of output in a year, it may be safe to assume that if demand for the product increases to 2 million units next year, then 20 workers would be required. Of course, these sorts of estimates will also need to be based on an understanding of the technologies used in production, and opportunities for reorganising work in a more efficient way.
2. **Work study techniques**. If the organisation has no existing measures of how much work is produced by individuals or groups of employees, then work study techniques can be helpful. Work study involves finding out how tasks can be performed more efficiently and timing the operation. By finding out how long it takes a typical employee to carry out an operation, then this figure can be multiplied by the total number of operations required to meet a particular production target – to work out total labour time and hence numbers of employees required.

The supply side of the Human Resource Plan

If an organisation is to work out the supply of labour available, then it must examine the numbers of people available to work, how long they can work for, their ability to do the required jobs, their productivity (output per head) and other factors (Figure 7).

Internal supply

Statistics and information need to be collected on employees already within the organisation. This will cover the following main areas:

- The number of employees in particular job categories. This figure will give a broad overview of the numbers in an organisation who already possess certain broad categories of skills, e.g. in a school this could be the number of staff qualified to teach history, geography, art, chemistry, etc. Or it could identify those who have had previous experience of teaching at A level, GCSE, etc.
- Skills available. It may be helpful to identify the current skills held by the labour force and to see how many of these are transferable (a skill used in a particular job may be able to be used in another job, e.g. an A level physics teacher may be able to teach some lower school mathematics).
- **Skills analysis.** An organisation needs to be sure that it has the right number of people available at the right time, but also

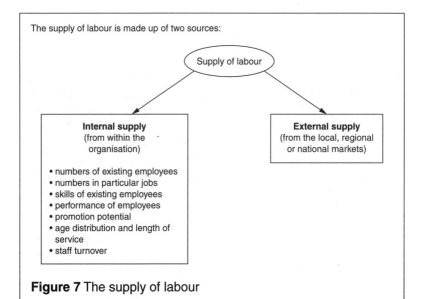

Figure 7 The supply of labour

with the right skills. Organisations therefore need to assess their present supply of skills across their workforce and to identify the sorts of skills they will require in the future. A **skills inventory** of current employees will indicate those who have received recent training and those who will require training. It may be possible to meet the human resource requirements of an organisation by training and developing current staff rather than recruiting externally (this is often a cheaper option and helps to motivate people that are already working for the organisation). For example, in schools, the National Curriculum has given increasing prominence to Information and Communications Technology (ICT). An existing subject teacher might like to go on a course to develop their ICT skills and to take on responsibility for co-ordinating ICT across the school. They may gain extra motivation from this process of 'job enlargement', i.e. taking on a wider range of responsibilities.

- **Performance results.** An organisation will want to gather information about the level of performance of various categories of current employees. This sort of information may be collected in a quantitative form, e.g. numbers of pupils passing GCSE history taught by a particular teacher comparing one year with the next. In addition, information may be collected which is of a qualitative nature, e.g. from a one-to-one interview between the Head of History and a particular history teacher.

- Promotion potential. It is useful to the organisation to know how many employees have the skills and aptitude for promotion to more demanding roles. In addition, it should know many employees have the potential, with suitable training to be promoted.

- Age distribution and length of service. Analysis of staff by age helps to identify possible problem areas. If the organisation has a high age profile then it might suddenly face a flood of retirements where it is difficult to replace the existing job holders. An organisation with too many young people may lack the experience required for effective decision making.

- Staff turnover. Staff turnover should be analysed in order to help an organisation to forecast future losses and to identify the reasons why people leave the organisation. A given degree of staff turnover may be advantageous as fresh staff can be recruited and promotion channels opened up. Too high a level of staff turnover will mean that there will be high additional costs of replacement, and recruitment and additional training costs.

Markov models

Markov models are sometimes used by Human Resource Planners to model the flow of individuals within an organisation. Markov models are based on the assumption that organisations have predictable wastage patterns (i.e. numbers of people leaving jobs) according to the length of service, and that this pattern can be picked out early in an individual's career. Once 'survival rates' have been calculated, a fairly stable pattern of progression and replacement needs over time can be worked out. It then becomes possible to predict future recruitment on the basis of stable patterns of wastage and promotion. The model can then be used not only for planning recruitment but also for training and development activities within the organisation.

Wastage rates

It is possible to calculate the number of staff who leave an organisation as a percentage of those who could have left.

$$\text{Wastage rate} = \frac{\text{Number of staff leaving in time period}}{\text{Average number of staff employed in time period}} \times 100$$

For example if a police force employs 1,000 police constables, 50 of whom leave the force each year, then the wastage rate would be:

$$\frac{50}{1000} \times 100 = 5\%.$$

Such information is used to predict likely turnover in the future, to establish the need to examine in detail reasons for high turnover and to establish the need to recruit new staff to replace those leaving. While the labour turnover index is useful, as with most statistics it needs to be considered alongside other factors. For example, are there particular areas of the organisation where the rate of leavers is high? It would also be useful to identify leavers' length of service (are the most experienced people leaving or people with relatively little experience?).

As well as the wastage rate, some organisations make use of a labour **stability index**. This provides an indication of the tendency for employees with long service to remain with the organisation, thus linking the leaving rate with the length of service.

$$\text{Stability index} = \frac{\text{Number of staff leaving with more than one year's service}}{\text{Number employed one year ago}} \times 100$$

External supply

The external labour market for any particular organisation is made up of potential employees, locally, regionally or nationally, who possess the skills and experience required at a particular time or who can be trained in these areas.

Important ingredients affecting the size and quality of this labour force include:

- the numbers of people currently available for work
- numbers that will be available in the future
- the skills, experience and aptitudes of potential employees
- the extent of competition from other organisations for these potential employees
- the age structure of the population, e.g. how many are in appropriate age ranges
- the existing and future levels of education and training for potential employees.

Steps in the Human Resource Planning process

In creating a Human Resources Plan organisations will need to consider the demand and supply of labour as outlined above. It is then possible to create a plan establishing how many and what kind of employees will be required in the future. Key steps in this planning process are as follows:

1. Setting up a Human Resource Planning Group in the organisation including key managers from across the organisation.
2. Setting out Human Resource Objectives for the organisation. These will be determined by such factors as the corporate plans for the organisation, the financial resources available for the organisation, likely future products and production levels, etc.
3. A detailed analysis of the present use of human resources in the organisation.
4. A detailed analysis of the external environment in which the organisation operates, e.g. government policies with regards to education and training, the availability of local housing, transport routes, etc.
5. The potential supply of labour.

The nature of the Human Resource Plan will depend on long-term corporate plans. Where the organisation is expanding and/or diversifying, then it will be looking towards recruitment and training strategies to take it forward.

Where the organisation is going through a period of stability it will tend to rely heavily on existing employees to see it through.

Where the organisation is downsizing, then its Human Resource Plans will be concerned with wastage and redundancies.

A Human Resource Audit

A **Human Resource Audit** is a discrete part of the Human Resource Plan which will set out the abilities, performance records and potential of each of the organisation's departments, as well as of employees. The aim of the audit is to match up the organisation's current and future human resources against current and forecast requirements.

By carrying out this exercise the organisation is able to set out a Human Resource Plan which sets out in detail, for each unit and sub-unit of the organisation how many employees and what types of employees it is practical to employ at various stages in the future.

The softer side of Human Resource Planning

In the past, manpower planning was very much a discipline which was carried out for the purposes of organisational efficiency. It prevented the embarrassment of finding that you were faced with some departments that were overstaffed with others being badly understaffed. It was usually a logistical and numerical exercise that could be carried out in a number crunching way.

More recently, Human Resource Planning has developed a softer side in which an emphasis is placed on meeting individual employee needs. This new approach is more in line with the notion of a psychological contract and enables the organisation both to meet its economic objectives and at the same time fulfil social responsibilities.

New perspectives on Human Resource Planning

In modern organisations where HRM is given a high priority the notion of Human Resource Planning involves far more than simply getting the right people in the right posts at the right time. Instead it relates to the whole process of devising **Human Resource Strategies** in the organisation and will be the responsibility of the Chief Executive Officer and staff, the chief Human Resource Officer and staff, and line managers and staff (Figure 8).

This strategic view of Human Resource Planning will involve the creation of an overarching plan to integrate the separate **Human Resource Activities** such as staffing, performance appraisal, compen-

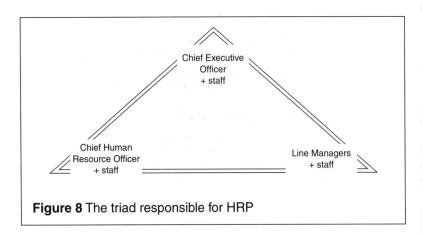

Figure 8 The triad responsible for HRP

sation and development. The strategic Human Resource Plan will be tied in to the corporate plan and business objectives of the organisation (Figure 9).

At the strategic planning stage, human resource planners will influence the organisation's philosophy, develop objectives for the human resource function, and shape strategies for carrying out the organisation philosophy and achieving the human resource objectives.

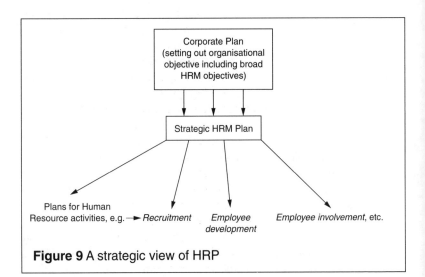

Figure 9 A strategic view of HRP

At the tactical planning stage, human resource planners develop structures for the allocation of resources in accordance with strategic Human Resource Objectives and Strategies.

Together, strategic and tactical planning for human resources provides guidance that will cause all members of an organisation to manage the human resources in a unified way.

The HRM strategy that an organisation selects will need to be founded in a clear philosophy which sets out the purpose of the organisation. One of the key purposes of the organisation will be to meet the needs of its people and this should translate into meeting the work-related needs of its employees in a variety of ways, including:

- quality of work life
- fulfilment
- belonging to an organisation one can be proud of
- job and career security.

KEY WORDS

Human Resource Planning	Skills analysis
Manpower planning	Skills inventory
Supply of labour	Performance results
Demands for labour	Markov models
Manpower flow	Wastage rates
Multi-skilling	Stability index
Job analysis	Human Resource Audit
Job descriptions	Human Resource Strategies
Person specifications	Human Resource Activities
Work study techniques	

Further reading

Cowling, A. and Mailer, C., Chapter 1 in *Managing Human Resources*, Arnold, 1998.

Foot, M. and Hook, C., Chapter 2 in *Introducing Human Resource Management*, Longman, 1999

Jarrell, D.W., Chapters 1–5 in *Human Resource Planning, A Business Planning Approach*, Prentice Hall, 1997.

Warr, P. (ed.), Chapter 12 in *Psychology at Work*, Penguin, 1998.

Further references

Porter, M.E., *Competitive Strategy*. New York: Free Press, 1980.

Essay topics

1. What steps does an organisation need to take to make sure that it has enough human resources of the right quality to meet its corporate plans? [25 marks]
2. What difficulties does an organisation face in predicting its future demand for labour, and the supply that will be available in the future? [10 marks] What steps might an organisation take to reduce this uncertainty? [15 marks]

Data response question

Culture change at Midland Exhausts

Midland Exhausts is an engineering company producing exhaust pipes which it sells mainly to emergency and rapid replacement exhaust workshops in the Midlands. The firm has produced exhaust pipes for many years and its traditional culture was based on a top-down model, with ground level employees being given very clear instructions from supervisors and line managers. However, during the 1980s the company came under strong pressure from rival firms, and needed to cut costs drastically in order to survive. The priority for Human Resource Planning was based very much on downsizing and so the company sought voluntary redundancies in its workforce in 1989.

In 1994 it was decided to change the way the company operated in order to improve operational efficiency. Small groups of employees were formed into teams with a team leader. The team leader needed to develop a democratic approach to decision making rather than giving orders. The teams were expected to take responsibility for their own work-based decisions and were made accountable for the results achieved – pay was linked to performance. Between 1994 and 2000 productivity per employee increased at an average annual rate of 5 per cent.

The figures in Table A on the following page show changes in employee turnover over the period in question.

Table A Changes in employee turnover

	1988	1989	1990	1991	1992	1993	1994	1995	1996	1997	1998	1999	2000
Average annual number of employees	650	480	450	400	400	400	400	400	400	410	420	430	440
Number of employees leaving during year	200	52	53	72	10	11	42	45	2	3	5	2	5 (est.)

1. Work out the employee turnover rate in each of the years shown. Set this information out on a graph. [10 marks]
2. How would you account for the fluctuations in employee turnover during the period shown? [5 marks]
3. How might human resource planners have taken steps to successfully manage the changes in numbers employed over the period shown? [10 marks]

Chapter Five

The employment procession

'A resource development approach can be used to encourage the integration of HRM across organisational activities. Using corporate strategy as the starting point organisations can generate "job models" which define in behavioural terms the criteria of competence at different levels and possibly in different functions of the enterprise. These job models can be used to inform the person specification when recruiting, to provide a reference point for appraisal sessions, to guide the construction of career maps and, possibly, to feed into reward systems. This model can be used to inform training. Such job models will identify fairly precisely what a person needs to bring to a given role in order to perform well, and these competencies can be linked directly to business strategy. Once defined in this way, competencies provide the opportunity to create consistency, coherence and mutual reinforcement across and with HRM policies and practices.'
R. Boam and P. Sparrow

One of the key responsibilities involved in managing people at work is that of managing the flow of new people into the organisation and retaining those that are already there. Human resource managers therefore have considerable responsibility for overseeing the successful running of a series of integrated activities, known as the **employment procession**. Some of these activities are shown in Figure 10.

Traditionally these activities were seen as the responsibility of the Personnel Department of an organisation. Today, the emphasis has shifted to seeing these activities as part of an integrated Human Resource Management strategy based on a consistent philosophy. The quote from Boam and Sparrow at the start of this chapter outlines

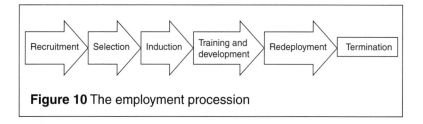

Figure 10 The employment procession

one way of creating integration – where using its strategic objectives as a guide an organisation can then develop a clear map of what people at each level in the organisation should be doing in their jobs. This understanding can then be used to inform a range of HRM policies and activities in an integrated rather than a fragmented way.

With the development of a strategic HRM approach in many organisations, these activities have increasingly been handed over to empowered line managers who are able to draw on the expertise, support, and the systems which have been created by HRM specialists. For example, a local bank branch might today carry out all or most of its own recruitment, selection and training activities using guidelines and by referring to policies established by the Head Office HRM team.

There are mixed accounts of the success of this devolution of powers in the organisation to the line manager. In some organisations the new HRM is extremely popular while in others it is met with cynicism.

Recruitment

Recruitment consists of:

- all those activities involved in identifying potential employees, and
- attracting applications from suitable prospective employees.

Key factors which will determine whether suitable candidates apply for a job vacancy are:

- the reputation of the company as a good employer
- the effectiveness of the advertising of the post
- the attractiveness of the salary and the conditions of service
- whether potential applicants think they can do the job
- whether the job looks interesting and satisfying.

Where companies have a reputation as a good employer they will find top candidates queuing up for a place in the company. Good companies regularly receive favourable press, so that prospective employees will know of the reputation of particular employers. Job advertising then needs to give clear messages about what particular jobs involve and to be placed in appropriate media, spelling out the details of salary and other conditions.

Recruitment

Recruitment should be a relatively straightforward, if time-consuming process: draw up a job description, work out the skills and attributes necessary for the position, then go and find the right person.

But it can't be as simple as that; for one thing, companies are not happy with the calibre of their own employees. In 1998 the human resources consultancy DDI polled HR directors from The Times Top 100 companies and found that, given the opportunity to recreate their workforce, only 60 per cent would rehire more than half their current employees.

In addition, some business sectors show worryingly high staff turnover rates. The Institute of Personnel and Development's 1997 labour survey looked at employee turnover rates in 22 business sectors and found rates in excess of 25 per cent in food and drink companies and consumer products. The average turnover figure was 15.85 per cent for full-time and 21.77 for part-time employees. The survey found the cost of replacing skilled workers to be £1652; for management just over £5,000. This is just the cost incurred after the decision to leave has been made; poor performers may have cost much more in lost output or business opportunities. Some consultants say the full cost of recruiting the wrong person can be four or five times the annual salary.

Aims of recruitment

The aims of recruitment must be to:

- make sure that all recruitment activities enhance the reputation of the company and contribute to corporate objectives (including HRM objectives).
- attract a pool of suitable applicants for particular posts.
- use and be seen to use a fair process – particularly meeting the required criteria for equal opportunities.
- ensure the best results in the most cost-effective way.

Recruitment policy

Organisations will need to develop a recruitment policy which is a clear written statement outlining the approach that everyone involved in the recruitment process is expected to take and the standards expected. The policy will set out both the goal of recruitment and the approaches employed to ensure fairness (i.e. equal opportunities).

Recruitment processes

There are a number of processes which are involved in the recruitment process, particularly in the creation of new jobs.

- **Job analysis**

This is the process of examining a job in detail in order to identify its component tasks. **Job analysis** can be conducted by direct observation of employees at work, by information obtained from interviewing job-holders, or by referring to documents such as training manuals. Information can be gleaned directly from the person carrying out a task and supervisory staff. Job analysis will involve describing the duties performed by a job holder, the most important duties, the time spent on each duty, how often the duties are carried out, the amount of supervision required, etc. The data from job analysis can then be used inform the creation of the **job description**.

- **Job description**

The job description will show how a particular employee is to fit into the organisation. Typically it will cover:

- the title of the job
- the reporting structure of the job, i.e. 'reports to X', 'is responsible for Y'
- the purpose of the job
- the major duties of the job.

Job descriptions can be used as reference points once a person is in post for clarifying the work and responsibilities that they are expected to carry out, and can be used for arbitrating in 'who does what' disputes.

- **Person specification**

The **person specification** sets out the skills and qualities a person would need to have to carry out the job well. For example, a job specification for a trainee manager's post in a retail store included the following:

> *Managers at all levels are expected to show responsibility. The company is looking for people who are tough and talented. They should have a flair for business, know how to sell, and to work in a team.*

The person specification will usually set out a list of essential and desirable characteristics that will be used in separating the strong from the weak candidates in the selection process.

- **Job advertisements**

Job advertisements are very important in selling the job and the company to prospective employees. The advertiser should seek to sell the job through the attractiveness and layout of the advert, the impression given of the company, training provided, pay, etc. Surveys typically show that potential candidates have the following priorities in scanning job advertisements:

- location of work
- salary
- closing date for applications
- how to apply
- experience required
- qualifications expected
- duties and responsibilities
- details about the organisation.

Selection

Selection simply involves choosing the right person for the job. Effective selection requires that the organisation makes the right prediction from data available about the various candidates for a post. Unfortunately organisations and individuals often make the wrong choice because they don't have enough data, or because they interpret the data in an inaccurate way.

Making the right choices in the selection process requires that the criteria used for selection are valid. **Criterion-related validity** is a measure of the relationship between performance on a selection test and performance on a set of job performance criteria. In other words the selection tests employed need to mirror real work requirements.

In contrast, **content-related validity** is where a selection test samples and measures the knowledge, skills or behaviours required to perform a job successfully.

The selection process therefore needs to involve valid selection instruments. Many studies show that interviews are not a very reliable selection technique because of their subjective nature (the way the interviewer views the candidate through their own perceptions and prejudices), because the interviewee can 'act' a part, and because the interview does not reflect the job to be performed.

As a result many modern selection procedures include a variety of tests, interviews, and simulations. Research indicates that the most valid form of selection method is the use of an assessment centre where candidates are subjected to a variety of tests including **interviews**, group exercises, presentations, **'in-tray' exercises**, and so on (Figures 11 and 12).

Psychometric (personality) tests have become increasingly popular in the UK in recent years and are often used alongside cognitive

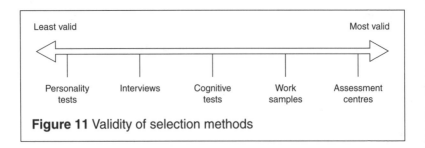

Figure 11 Validity of selection methods

(reasoning) tests. Psychometric tests can be used to identify the personality of an individual – whether they are extrovert or introvert, whether they are creative or methodical, etc. Personality testing has become increasingly important with the development of teamwork approaches in modern organisations, because people need to have some level of compatibility to pull together.

Interviews will be most successful when they are tightly related to job analysis, job description and the person specification. Using 'essential' and 'desirable' criteria makes selection more clear cut. If there are seven essentials, then those candidates that don't have all seven don't fit the role.

Work samples can be employed as a certain way of knowing whether candidates can perform a job, but the process can be long and drawn out if there are a lot of candidates to be compared. In some occupations candidates for a job may be asked to show a sample of their work, e.g. a teaching applicant may be asked to give a short talk.

In-tray exercises can be used for candidates to respond to work-related and other problems which are presented to them in an in-tray to be processed.

For the process to be effective it is essential that the candidates are familiarised with the nature of the work they will be doing, and the organisation they will be working for.

Induction

Induction is concerned with helping a new employee to fit into a new job, and often into a new organisation. Employees are far more likely to resign during their first few months than at any subsequent time, particularly during times of high employment. Some of this is attributable to people finding out they are in the wrong job – which relates as much to the selection procedure as the induction process. But a large part can be put down to 'trouble fitting in'.

Companies working towards **Investors in People** (IiP) accreditation

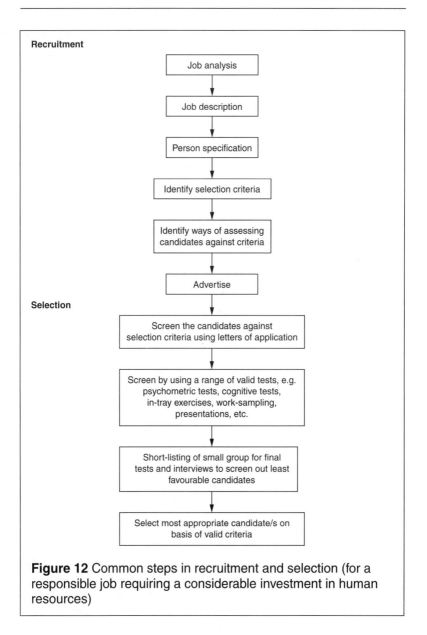

Recruitment

Job analysis

Job description

Person specification

Identify selection criteria

Identify ways of assessing
candidates against criteria

Advertise

Selection

Screen the candidates against
selection criteria using letters of application

Screen by using a range of valid tests, e.g.
psychometric tests, cognitive tests,
in-tray exercises, work-sampling,
presentations, etc.

Short-listing of small group for final
tests and interviews to screen out least
favourable candidates

Select most appropriate candidate/s on
basis of valid criteria

Figure 12 Common steps in recruitment and selection (for a
responsible job requiring a considerable investment in human
resources)

must include their induction procedures. IiP requires that 'all new
employees are introduced effectively to the organisation and all
employees new to a job are given the **training** and development they
need to do that job'.

Induction marks the start of the relationship between employer and employee and is of fundamental importance in setting standards and patterns of behaviour. Good inductions have three main objectives:

1. To help employees settle in to their new environment.
2. To help employees understand their responsibilities.
3. To ensure that the organisation receives the benefit of a well trained and motivated employee as quickly as possible.

The induction process should actually start when a job applicant is interviewed for a post. The interview process should ensure that both parties know what they are letting themselves in for. Potential recruits can be given a tour of the place of work and have rules and procedures explained to them.

There are major advantages in providing induction material in advance of the joining day. It calms nerves, smoothes the transition into the new workplace and can speed the induction process by helping the new employee to prepare. As well as the basics like conditions of employment, job descriptions and instructions about the first day at work, the pre-employment pack can contain staff handbooks, house journals and press cuttings.

The first priority on joining is to give the new recruit up-front information that is critical to health and safety and to basic comfort (terms and conditions, payroll, location of toilets, food and drink). Right from the start new employees need to feel welcomed.

There is a growing trend in the UK for induction to take place in shorter bursts, interspersed with work in the new job but covering a longer period of employment. This fits in better with the notion of lifetime learning, and there is a limit to how much inductees can absorb at any one time. Most induction packages include a period of formal instruction, and team-based activities for new employees, coupled with induction that includes some form of work shadowing or 'buddy' system whereby the inductee spends some time with a more experienced employee.

Training and development

Training includes all forms of planned learning experiences and activities which are designed to make positive changes to performance and other behaviour involving the acquisition of new knowledge, skills, beliefs, values and attitudes. Learning is generally defined as 'a relatively permanent change in behaviour that occurs as a result of practice and experience'.

Organisations carry out a **Training Needs Analysis** (TNA) to identify and compare actual levels of performance of the organisation with desired levels of performance (i.e. the competencies and attitudes necessary for employees to do the job to the required standard). By comparing current levels of performance with future desired levels of performance it is possible to identify any shortfall, which can be made up through training. As time moves on the organisation will require new competencies and attitudes.

Sparrow and Bognanno (1993) identify four types of competency which help the organisation to analyse the need for training in its workforce:

- **Emerging competencies** are those that are becoming more important as the organisation follows its new strategies.
- **Maturing competencies** are those that are becoming out of date.
- **Transitional competencies** are those that are required by employees in a period of change (e.g. the ability to cope with uncertainty and stress).
- **Stable or core competencies** are those that are central to the organisation's performance on a continuing basis.

Figure 13 shows how competence requirements change in an organisation as it moves from the present into the future. Identifying the future competence requirements of the organisation will help human resource managers and hence line managers in an organisation to identify appropriate training solutions, as well as to produce a range of other solutions to meet the organisation's ongoing requirements such as job specifications and activities designed to change the way in which individuals operate within an organisation – for example,

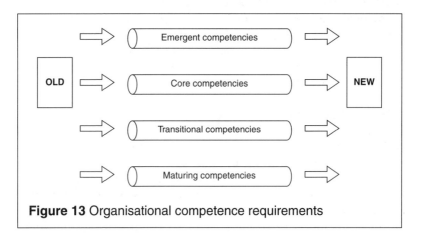

Figure 13 Organisational competence requirements

to help them to work better within the changing culture of an organisation, perhaps through teamwork development.

Development approaches individuals and their motivation from a different angle to that of training. While training is typically concerned with enabling individuals to contribute better to meeting the objectives of the organisation, personal development is more concerned with enabling individuals to develop themselves in the way that bests suits individual needs. Hopefully the two will come together. By helping individuals to develop themselves they will be more inclined and better able to contribute to helping the organisation to meet its objectives.

The organisation that just concentrates on its own objectives without thinking about the needs of its employees is a selfish organisation. The individual employee who simply thinks about their own development needs without considering how these can support the organisation in meeting its own objectives is a selfish employee.

Personal professional development should be the responsibility of the individual concerned. There can be no 'personal' development without individuals taking ownership for their own development and choosing how such development will take place. However, the organisation needs to support individuals in effectively developing themselves. The prime opportunity for the organisation to find out about individual development needs is through the appraisal interview. Through appraisal the organisation is able to communicate its objective to the person being appraised, while the individual employee is able to clarify their development needs.

Promotion, transfer and termination

Developing policies and procedures to move human resources to different positions of responsibility and to widen their experience through transfers, as well as termination of employment, is an important area of human resource work. Again, these areas need to be covered in ways which are consistent with the integrated HRM approach and in line with corporate strategy. **Promotion** is an important vehicle for motivation within the organisation and the mapping out of career progression within an organisation will help to create commitment to the organisation. Line managers have an important part to play in supporting the development process for individual employees. **Transfers** may take place to smooth out difficulties in the work environment or to provide individuals with a broader range of experience.

Termination of employment may be the result of resignation, retirement, dismissal or redundancy. In line with HRM philosophy termination is as important as any other part of the job procession. Effective HRM requires that employees are cared for from the start of their life with an organisation to the finish. Poor practice in this area will have a demoralising effect on the individuals concerned and across the organisation as a whole.

KEY WORDS

Job models	Work samples
Employment procession	Induction
Recruitment	Investors in People
Job analysis	Training
Job description	Training Needs Analysis
Person specification	Emerging competencies
Job advertisement	Maturing competencies
Selection	Transitional competencies
Criterion-related validity	Stable or core competencies
Content-related validity	Development
Interviews	Promotion
In-tray exercise	Transfers
Psychometric tests	Termination

Further reading

Cowling, A. and Mailer, C. (eds), Chapters 2, 3 and 4 in *Managing Human Resources*, Arnold, 1998.

Dransfield, R. *et al.*, Chapters 7, 11 and 12 in *Human Resource Management for Higher Awards*, Heinemann, 1996.

Foot, M. and Hook, C., Chapters 3, 4, 5, 6, 7 and 8 in *Introducing Human Resource Management*, Longman, 1999.

Warr, P. (ed.), Chapters 5 and 12 in *Psychology at Work*, Penguin, 1998.

Further references

Boam, R. and Sparrow, P., *Designing and Achieving Competency*. Maidenhead: McGraw-Hill, 1992.

Bognanno, M., 'Facilitating cultural change by identifying the new competencies required and formulating a strategy to develop such competencies', Conference on identifying and applying competencies in your organisation, Nov 6, 1990, London, IIP.

Useful websites

Investors in People – in 1993 the Investors in People (IiP) national quality standard was created, which sets a level of good practice for improving an organisation's performance through its people; website includes information about the standard: www.iipuk.co.uk/

Information about Human Resource Management subjects, produced by Ray Lye, a lecturer at Nottingham Business School: www.nbs.ntu.ac.uk/staff/lyerj/hrm-link_htm

International recruitment agency Price Jamieson – jobs are updated weekly: www.gold.net/PriceJam/

The Kiersey Temperament sorter – provides an interesting approach to assessing personality; an on-screen questionnaire to complete which you are then able to score: www.kiersey.com/cgibin/kiersey/newkts.cgi

Essay questions

1. (a) Should organisations treat activities in the recruitment procession in an integrated way? [12 marks]
   (b) How could they achieve this integration? [13 marks]
2. (a) Explain how an organisation can attract 'the right people' to fill particular jobs. [12 marks]
   (b) How can the organisation then ensure that the people it selects continues to be 'the right people'? [13 marks]

Data response question

The information on the following page is given to employees starting work at the Head Office of a major confectionery company.

Starter's Information – Head Office

1. Documents	ALL documents should be handed to your local Human Resources Department for copying, i.e. exam certificates, birth certificate, P45, driving licence, contract, Pension Nomination Form.
2. Security	All visitors must report to reception. ID pass MUST BE WORN AT ALL TIMES.
3. Lifts	Front Lifts: Express: First stop is 11th floor, then from 11th to 22nd.
	Back Lifts: Slow: Ground to 11th floor (behind reception).
4. Health and safety	
General	Remember always to take reasonable care of your own health and safety and that of others around you.
Fire and evacuation	If you discover a fire, sound the alarm immediately. Leave the building by the nearest safe exit – DO NOT use lifts. Go to assembly point in front of building. On hearing the fire alarm, leave the building by the nearest safe exit and go to assembly point.
Occupational health department (OHD)	Location A24. Open 8.30 a.m. to 5.30 p.m., Mon–Fri. Occupational Health Nurses and the Medical Officer are available to provide advice and assistance on many aspects of health and safety, including counselling.
Accident and injury reporting	Report all accidents, dangerous incidents and safety related problems or defects to your line manager or other responsible person as soon as possible.
	If you sustain an injury at work, no matter how minor, report to the OHD or your local first aider for treatment.
Illness at work	If you become ill at work, inform your line manager and report to the OHD.
	Following illness, anyone involved with the handling of food MUST report to the OHD before entering any food preparation areas.
Sickness reporting	If you are unable to attend work, it is your responsibility to inform your line manager within one hour of your start time.
5. Restaurant	Open 12 noon to 2.00 p.m. Facilities for permanent and temporary employees only. Personal guests not permitted. Self-service, hot meals, snack bar, salad bar, all subsidised.
6. Company shop	Stocks most company confectionery products. Open 12 noon to 2 p.m., and 4.00 p.m. to 5.00 p.m. every working day.
7. Fitness centre	Fitness centre located on ground floor. Full multigym and shower facilities.
	Not available to staff during core hours. Opening time 7.30 a.m. to 7.00 p.m every working day.
8. Staff notice boards	Staff notice boards are situated on each floor with information on job vacancy lists, announcements, company information, etc.
9. Company news	In-house magazine produced bi-monthly.
10. Season tickets	Interest free loans are available for annual local car parking and train season tickets (monthly deductions from payroll). Contact Human Resource Management Department for details.
11. Change of particulars	Please inform the Human Resource Department of your extension number and location address as soon as you are in your new department and any change to your personal circumstances, e.g. change of address, emergency contact, etc.
12. Pay day	Your salary will be paid into a nominated bank/building society account on the 21st of each month.

1. Why is the document above produced by the Human Resources Department in an organisation? [5 marks]
2. At what stage in the induction process would it be best to provide the new employee with this document? [3 marks]
3. What is the purpose of the document? [2 marks]
4. How effective do you think the document is in helping the inductee? [5 marks]
5. Which of the information shown on the document would need to be additionally addressed as part of the induction process? [5 marks]
6. To what extent do you think the document shows that the confectionery company concerned is using a Human Resource Management perspective? [5 marks]

Chapter Six

Performance management

'Performance management is a process which is designed to improve organisational, team and individual performance and which is owned and driven by line managers.'
Michael Armstrong

Performance management is an HRM process (which has become increasingly popular since the 1980s) concerned with getting the best performance from individuals in an organisation, as well as getting the best performance from teams, and the organisation as a whole. Effective performance management therefore involves sharing an understanding of what needs to be achieved and then managing and developing people in a way that enables such shared objectives to be achieved.

3M Corporate Objectives 1998

The following is taken from 3M's Corporate Objectives for 1998, and shows how the organisation has set out to give clear direction at corporate level to inform HRM objectives and individual performance objectives:

'3M management believes that it is essential to provide an organisational structure and work climate which respects the dignity and worth of individuals, encourages initiative, challenges individual capacities, provides equal opportunities for development and equitably rewards efforts and contribution. It will endeavour to provide a stable work environment which promotes career employment. It believes 3M employees are the corporation's most valuable source.'

The ideal situation for an organisation is to have everyone pulling in the same direction. Supporters of the HRM approach argue that this two-way process will only be effective where there is a clear psychological contract between employers and employees based on mutual trust and commitment. The organisation will benefit from setting out its aims in a clear way, for example by having a **mission statement** (a brief statement setting out general aims) which then gives direction to effort at every level in the organisation.

The mission statement might read like the following:

'Super-Supermarkets sets out to provide its customers with the best value for money family shopping coupled with unrivalled quality service, based on the commitment and efforts of all our people.'

Coupled with this, the organisation will create a **values statement** such as:

'Super-Supermarkets believes in putting service at the forefront of everything we do. We are a caring company based on a teamwork ethic, while valuing the individual and their contribution.'

Given the mission and values, the organisation can create **performance objectives** at every level within the organisation right down to personal objectives for individual members of the organisation. The performance of an organisation, teams, and individuals in the organisation can all be measured and compared against objectives. Peter Drucker used the term **Management by Objectives** (MbO) to identify a management approach which involves the establishment of clear objectives and the subsequent measurement of performance against these objectives (Figure 14). Objectives may need to be adjusted in the light of performance (e.g. where objectives are too easy or hard to attain).

In recent years MbO has become less popular with HRM specialists because of its essentially managerial perspective, and because of difficulties and dangers associated with too rigid definitions of objectives at a time when creative solutions to problems from employees are being sought, based on an empowered approach to work.

A well-developed performance management system will include the following:

- a statement outlining the organisation's values
- a statement of the organisation's objectives
- individual objectives which are linked to the organisation's objectives
- regular performance reviews throughout the year
- performance-related pay
- training and counselling.

With such a system in place it becomes possible to establish for a period of time the **Key Results Areas** that an individual will be judged against. The results individuals achieve can then be judged against expected standards. A reward system can then be tailored to the way in which the individual enables the organisation to achieve its results.

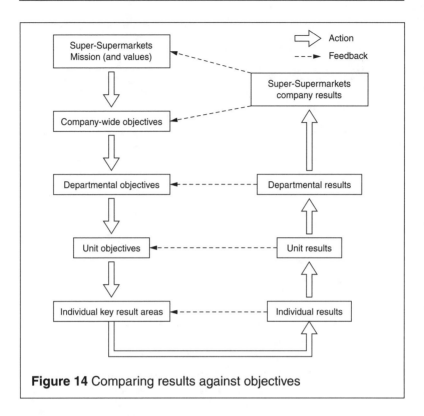

Figure 14 Comparing results against objectives

Performance appraisal

Performance appraisal is a process of systematically evaluating perform-ance and providing feedback on which performance adjustments can be made. Performance appraisal works on the basis of the following formula:

Desired performance – Actual performance = Need for action

A useful definition of performance appraisal is set out by the Advisory, Conciliation and Arbitration Service (ACAS) which states that:

'appraisals regularly record an assessment of an employee's performance, potential and development needs. The appraisal is an opportunity to take an overall view of work content, loads and volume, to look back on what has been achieved during the reporting period and agree objectives for the next'.

Different views on appraisal

Appraisal is an issue which is hotly debated. Some people believe that appraisal should be used strictly for development purposes. Appraisal should be used to review constructively individuals' performances in order to encourage them. Linking it to reward linked processes spoils the appraisal process because it then makes appraisal judgemental, punitive, and frightening. It is not only the person being appraised that suffers in such a situation but also the appraiser who plays the role of judge and executioner.

In contrast, many other people feel that appraisal should be linked closely to performance issues and to rewards.

The appraisal as development approach is most closely associated with soft HRM, while the appraisal with performance and rewards approach is associated with hard HRM.

Most organisations will attempt to convey the standards of performance and behaviour that they require from their employees by communicating them in job descriptions, competency statements, or performance objectives. Accurate assessment can only be achieved if appraisers and appraisees are both very clear about what criteria will be used in determining how strong or weak the performance is. Appraisal that does not have this foundation is likely to be very subjective and devoid of any clear direction for future development.

The major purposes of performance appraisal are to:

1. define the specific job criteria against which performance will be measured
2. measure past job performance accurately
3. justify the rewards given to individuals and/or groups, thereby discriminating between high and low performers
4. define the development experiences that the person being appraised needs to enhance their performance in the present job, and to prepare them for future responsibilities.

New forms of appraisal

Traditional forms of appraisal are associated with a 'top-down' model of appraisal by a supervisor, or line manager. However, in the modern world of empowerment and team working in organisations there are all sorts of variants.

Figure 15 on page 74 shows some of the possible sources of appraisal for the manager (at the centre of the diagram). In the 1990s

---

Useful guidelines for appraisal

- Arrange a confidential appointment, allowing sufficient time to prepare.
- Prior to the interview, both the appraiser and the appraisee should gather information that helps to identify indicators to strengths, weaknesses and training needs.
- At the interview the appraiser should try to put the appraisee at ease.
- Agree the objectives of the interview: clarify and agree that current performance is under review; stress that both of you have much to learn.
- Stress the developmental nature of the exercise and show how the interview is of value to both the appraisee and the institution. Ask the appraisee to suggest what hopes they have for the discussion.
- Ask the appraisee for positive and negative comments, i.e. what things they have done well and what things could be improved.
- Agree outcomes; explain how a summary will be agreed and plans formulated for future needs and development; the appraisee may take notes if they wish.
- Review job description and past performance following the rules of giving constructive feedback.
- Identify training needs.
- Agree an action plan.
- Ask the appraisee for final comments.
- End on a positive note; thank the appraisee and show appreciation for their effort; identify the time for the next appraisal.

Common stages of staff appraisal

1. Line manager meets with the job holder to discuss what is expected. The agreed expectations might be expressed in terms of targets, performance standards or required job behaviours – attributes, skills and attitudes.
2. The outcome of the meeting is recorded and usually signed by both parties.
3. The job holder performs the job for a set period of time.
4. At the end of this period, the job holder and the line manager or team leader meet again to review and discuss progress made. They draw up new action plans to deal with identified problems and agree targets and standards for the next period.

---

the notion of 360-degree appraisal became popular, whereby a manager might receive feedback on performance from below, above, and sideways.

Self-evaluation and peer evaluation

Self-evaluation and peer evaluation have become increasingly important in HRM work as a result of the empowerment process and the spread of team working. Self-evaluation involves employees establishing meaningful goals and then evaluating their own performance

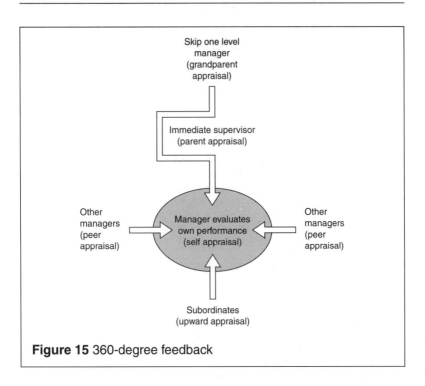

Figure 15 360-degree feedback

in meeting these goals. Employees who are given work assignments to do are also often encouraged to evaluate their own performance in carrying out these assignments to the required standard.

Self-evaluation
Benefits of self-evaluation are as follows:

1. The employee takes more responsibility for their own work area and for monitoring their own performance in this area. This is motivational.
2. The employee may have a greater understanding of their own work area, and the job than an external appraiser may have. This is increasingly the case where employees are working in highly creative, individual situations, developing interpersonal relations which are not always easy to scrutinise and measure.
3. Self-evaluation is cost-effective. It avoids the wasteful expense (including time) of having external evaluators.
4. Self-evaluation enables individuals to develop a much clearer picture of exactly what it is that they are doing – making work definition much better.

Peer evaluation
Peer evaluation involves assessment by employees at the same level in an organisation who are often part of the same work team or Quality Circle. Peer group evaluation makes it possible to check on how much team members are contributing to the product of the teamwork (i.e. the work results of the team effort) and to the process of the teamwork (i.e. helping the team to work effectively as a high performance team).

Peer evaluation can be very effective in that it creates a collaborative approach at work. People don't feel that they are being judged from above. There are a number of ingredients which help peer evaluation to be a success, including:

- respect for each other
- trust in each other
- non-competitive atmosphere
- willingness to take risks
- confidentiality
- willingness to listen and give full attention
- confidence to express views openly
- willingness to value each other's contribution
- participation by all members
- honesty
- no interruptions by participants
- confidence of participants to challenge each other.

Unfortunately, peer evaluation can often result in low levels of criticism so that performance is judged in too favourable a light. Also peer evaluation can create an approach whereby those that work in the peer evaluation system build up a defensive position against the organisation – to justify their own decisions and performance, rather than viewing things from the organisation's side.

Monitoring performance
By reviewing an individual's previous performance and weighing up their strengths and level of effort it is possible to identify areas where further development would be helpful. The emphasis should be on improving future performance.

There are three broad approaches to staff appraisal, based on personal attributes, skills or performance. Schemes will often contain elements of all three. A large organisation may use different schemes for different groups of employees.

Personal attributes

The designers of the appraisal scheme identify the personal attributes that affect job performance, for example:

- reliability
- judgement
- application
- initiative
- adaptability.

There are several criticisms of this approach. For example, the attributes are open to wide interpretation by the many managers undertaking appraisal in different parts of the organisation.

Skills

The appraisal focuses on the employee's proficiency in the skills relevant to the particular job. These might include technical competence, such as operating particular equipment; communication skills, such as report writing; and interpersonal skills needed to deal with customers. The person doing the appraisal, usually the manager, observes the employee over a period of time and records their judgement of the employee's competence.

Performance

The basis of appraisal is the achievement of agreed performance standards or targets. Supporters of this approach point to its objectivity. However, it is difficult in some jobs to find a satisfactory measure of individual performance – for example, how would you measure the performance of a nurse? Another problem is that of isolating the performance of individuals from that of the team they work for.

Measuring individual and group performance

Often within organisations there is a considerable amount of dissatisfaction about the way different individuals or groups are rewarded in the system which may seem to defy logic.

Behaviour scales

Many appraisal schemes include **behaviour scales** because it is felt that behaviour rather than personality should be appraised and rewarded.

Behaviour scales describe a range of behaviours that contribute to a greater or lesser degree to the successful achievement of the cluster of tasks which make up a job. Supervisors carrying out an appraisal are asked to indicate which statements on the specially designed form most accurately describe a subordinate's behaviour. A detailed version of this is the **Behaviourally Anchored Rating Scales** (**BARS**). Statements about work behaviour are used to create scales, which must then be tested to confirm their relevance and accuracy.

Competencies

Today many organisations use a competency-based approach to measuring performance. **Competency** is defined as 'an underlying characteristic of an individual which is related to effective or superior performance in a job'. The notion of competency is not new – Hugh Heffner who set up *Playboy* magazine used competencies to train 'bunny girls' who worked for him.

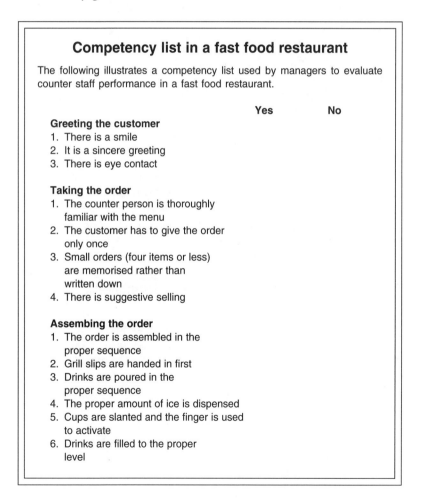

Competency list in a fast food restaurant

The following illustrates a competency list used by managers to evaluate counter staff performance in a fast food restaurant.

	Yes	No

Greeting the customer
1. There is a smile
2. It is a sincere greeting
3. There is eye contact

Taking the order
1. The counter person is thoroughly familiar with the menu
2. The customer has to give the order only once
3. Small orders (four items or less) are memorised rather than written down
4. There is suggestive selling

Assembing the order
1. The order is assembled in the proper sequence
2. Grill slips are handed in first
3. Drinks are poured in the proper sequence
4. The proper amount of ice is dispensed
5. Cups are slanted and the finger is used to activate
6. Drinks are filled to the proper level

Job evaluation is the process of assessing in an organisation the value of one job in relation to another, without regard to the ability of personality of the individuals currently holding the position. It results in a pay range for each job. An individual's personal worth is recognised by awarding increments within the fixed range for the job.

Merit rating

Merit rating is a system whereby the individual employee is awarded increments or bonuses based on a systematic appraisal of their developed skill level and performance. Merit rating usually operates within a job-evaluated pay structure. Job evaluation sets the pay bands while merit rating determines the position of the individual within the band.

A typical pattern is as follows:

- Starter: degree of efficiency expected from a learner.
- Qualified: able to perform normal aspects of the job.
- Experienced: able to deal with all circumstances of the job.
- Superior: ready for promotion, equivalent to starter of the next grade.

Performance-related Pay (PRP)

Automatic increases within fixed pay bands have largely disappeared. The trend is towards performance-related pay as the preferred method of deciding non-manual workers' progress through their salary bands. Merit-rating schemes, in the past, often relied on managers' subjective assessments of employees' personal characteristics. The increments, if awarded were usually stepped and fixed. PRP schemes use performance and/or competence as the criteria for deciding the size of increments and therefore also the rate of progress through a salary band. The PRP approach is based on a Management-by-Objectives philosophy of agreeing:

- the key results areas of the job
- clear standards of performance and target levels of competence
- regular, objective reviews of performance and competence

As a result of the PRP review the manager might, for example, assess an employee as outstanding, superior, standard or developing. The percentage pay increase awarded would then be influenced by:

- typical rates of pay for employees in that industry/occupational grouping at a particular time
- the financial state of the company

- the present position of the employee in the salary band
- company policy on speed of progress through the salary band.

Linking performance reviews and evaluations to training and development

It is important to stress that the process of appraisal and other forms of evaluation should be closely linked to training and development. This is a two-way process – if the organisation is to achieve its objectives, then it is essential to train and develop its people so that they are best able to support the organisation in working towards objectives. At the same time the individual needs to have the opportunity to be able to communicate their own personal development needs to the organisation through appraisal or personal development planning schemes. Many employers will use the appraisal process as a key part of their human resource planning process, or for individual career development plans. Individuals will be identified who can make important contributions to the ongoing development of the organisation. **Personal development plans** should be drawn up as a part of and as a result of the appraisal process enabling individuals to set out their own short- and long-term plans for development. Individual development plans can then be linked into team and organisational development plans.

Helping individuals to improve performance – mentoring and coaching

It has become increasingly popular for organisations to support individuals to improve performance by assigning a mentor or coach to that individual. Both **mentoring** and **coaching** involve an experienced hand helping a learner to become more effective in their role. However, there are four key differences between mentoring and coaching:

- Mentoring is a long, if intermittent, relationship; while coaching can cover a long time span, it can also be limited to a single session.
- Coaching is a valuable skill for line managers; the mentoring role, by contrast, is separate from that of line manager and the same person should not carry out both.
- The mentoring relationship is more about context than content: it's less concerned with day-to-day work than with longer-term issues such as working relationships and career paths.
- Coaching can be public – groups of people can be coached, mentoring is conducted in confidence on a one-to-one basis.

Coaching at Glaxo Wellcome

In 1998 Glaxo Wellcome used coaching as part of a change programme for senior managers. The organisation needed to get closer to its customers, so managers had to change from command-and-control to empowering employees to make decisions for themselves. This required a change in management attitudes.

Each manager was assigned a coach. Each pair had six to eight one-to-one sessions, each two or three hours long, over a six-month period. The manager set the goals, but it was up to the coach to guide the process. After each session the managers worked on the subject just covered, and reported on progress next time. One subject covered was coaching skills. Success was measured by feedback from those who reported to the managers: What has changed for you? What parts of your job have grown? In the majority of cases, results were favourable.

Within HRM there is a clash of perspectives as to whether appraisal should be seen primarily as a tool to enhance individual development within the organisation (a soft HRM approach), or as one to make sure that the organisation's objectives are being pursued by everyone in the organisation, and that levels of performance in meeting objectives should be differentially rewarded (a hard HRM approach). The two perspectives typically represent alternative views on motivation – the soft approach encouraging intrinsic motivation, and the hard approach extrinsic motivation. A system of performance management will not succeed in bringing about high performance against objectives unless employees consciously act in ways seen as being most likely to achieve the objectives. Expectancy theory sets out the need to tie performance outcomes to rewards which are valued by employees (if employees expect to receive rewards which they regard as being desirable, then they will seek to perform well to secure the rewards). In contrast, goal-setting theory lays stress on the need for acceptance by employees of the goals in themselves, so that motivation is more intrinsically based.

Communications in Human Resource Management

It should be clear that successful HRM will only be successful in organisations where good communications systems exist. HRM involves the opening up of channels of communication within the organisation, moving away from a **top-down flow of communications** to a **multi-channel communications process** (Figure 16).

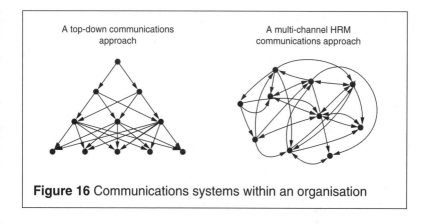

Figure 16 Communications systems within an organisation

In an HRM-driven organisation typical internal methods of communication will include the following:

- **Team briefings** – in which team leaders, supervisors and managers communicate developments and plans to their work teams.
- **Team meetings** – in which work teams discuss work related issues. The spread of teamworking has become widespread as the result of the 'Japanisation' of large sectors of UK manufacturing industry in the 1990s and early 2000s. For example, at the Jaguar car plant in Castle Bromwich, teams of production line workers each have a base alongside the production line where they regularly meet to discuss work related issues and to suggest improvements as part of the 'kaizen' process.
- Employee newsletters – keeping people up to date with what is happening in the organisation, and broadcasting the achievements of individuals and teams.
- Bulletin boards, often outlining in a pictorial form latest developments in the whole organisation, or part of an organisation, as well as identifying training and development opportunities.
- Electronic communication systems, such as shared databases and e-mail systems to network communications, and to provide up-to-the-minute communications.
- Training updates – training sessions which provide opportunities to communicate state-of-the-art developments in the organisation, and changes in practice.

During the 1990s there was an increasing trend in UK organisational practice to move away from a top-down communications model to a teamworking model. This has required a radical change in management approaches and styles away from a 'telling' approach towards a 'consultative' approach. Managers have therefore had to develop listening skills, and the ability to encourage others to communicate their own ideas.

KEY WORDS

Performance management	Job evaluation
Mission statement	Merit rating
Values statement	Performance-related Pay
Performance objectives	Personal development plans
Management by Objectives	Mentoring
Key Results Areas	Coaching
Performance Appraisal	Top-down flow of
360-degree appraisal	communications
Self-evaluation	Multi-channel communications
Peer evaluation	process
Behaviour scales	Team briefings
Behaviourably Anchored	Team meetings
Rating Scales (BARS)	Telling approach
Competency	Consulting approach

Further reading

Cowling, A. and Mailer, C., Chapter 10 in *Managing Human Resources*, Arnold, 1998.

Dransfield, R. *et al.*, Chapters 5, 18 and 20 in *Human Resource Management for Higher Awards*, Heinemann, 1996.

Foot, M. and Hook, C., Chapter 9 in *Introducing Human Resource Management*, Longman, 1999.

Myland, L., 'Problems with appraisals', *Training Journal*, April 1999, pp. 18–19.

Further references

Armstrong, M., *Performance Management*. Kogan Page, 1994.

Useful website

Some useful perspectives on performance appraisal produced by Archer North & Associates: www.performance-appraisal.com/intro.htm

Essay topics

1. How can the appraisal process best be used to ensure that the organisation's and the individual's objectives are closely linked. [25 marks]

2. 'Performance appraisal should be seen as a development tool, rather than being narrowly linked to rewards.' Discuss this assertion. [25 marks]

Data response question

Questionnaire reveals what the workers think

By 1997, 10 per cent of larger organisations in the UK had adopted the process of 360-degree feedback, and 50 per cent of non-user companies said that they planned to introduce it by 2000.

The idea behind 360-degree feedback isn't hard to grasp. The process aims to paint a complete picture of an individual's performanc by asking colleagues who work above and below them to comment on their at-work behaviour. The individual completes a questionnaire (either on paper, disk or online), while a second version of the questionnaire is filled in by various 'stakeholders'. A feedback report is then generated and the individual is asked to review their results with their line manager and/or with a trained facilitator.

'360-degree feedback should never be used as a pay and punishment instrument – it is about feedback and improvement,' stressed one manager in a large healthcare company. This is the standard corporate line. Yet although mainly used as a personal development tool tied into corporate strategy, the prospect of a 10-page questionnaire followed by a one-to-one 'interrogation' can make the most experienced manager suspect the onset of a Big Brother culture, and send him or her scurrying to scour the job ads.

Alarmingly, employees in three-quarters of user companies have felt threatened by introduction of the process, according to a new report by the Institute of Personnel and Development. 'The organisations that succeed are those which encourage an open culture, where giving and receiving feedback at all levels is seen as normal and nothing to be afraid of,' explains Imogen Daniels of the IPD. Some companies have failed because they haven't properly taken into account the issues of confidentiality and management of feedback.

Adapted from an article in the *Independent on Sunday*, 16 January 2000

1. How might 360-degree feedback support organisations in meeting their corporate objectives? [6 marks]
2. What are the prime benefits of 360-degree feedback? [4 marks] Who gets these benefits? [3 marks]
3. What criticisms might be levelled at 360-degree feedback? [6 marks]
4. On balance is the concept of 360-degree feedback part of Human Resource Management? [6 marks]

Chapter Seven
Employee relations

'If the trade union movement is to reverse its decline, there must be a major re-think of its priorities, structures and organisation. And the argument for a new form of industrial relations, built on social partnership, must be won.'
John Monks, General Secretary of the Trades Union Congress

Introduction
Employee relations is concerned with:

- the different and shared interests of employers and employees
- the processes through which their different interests are reconciled and the terms of that reconciliation as expressed in agreements
- the relative balance of bargaining power and how this influences management's employee relations policies and practices.

The main aspects of employee relations can therefore be illustrated in Figure 17.

The disappearance of the 'old model' of employee relations
During the 1970s the term 'employee relations' was largely associated with dealings between trade unions and employers. Trade unions had far greater influence in a period in which large numbers of people were still employed in large-scale manufacturing industries.

Since 1979 the numbers of employees who are members of trade unions have fallen steadily from over 55 per cent in 1979 to less than 40 per cent by 1995. Trade union membership dropped by 20 per cent between 1990 and 1997. However, figures published in 1999 indicate that this fall in union membership may have bottomed out. The Trades Union Congress's (TUC) figures for January 1999 showed the first increase for 19 years (from 6.64 million to 6.75 million in 1998). This bottoming out was backed up with figures from the government's labour force survey in which individuals were interviewed to self-assess whether they were members of trade unions; the figures showed the smallest annual fall in union membership for ten years.

Union density measures actual trade union membership as a percentage of potential union membership and recent figures show that

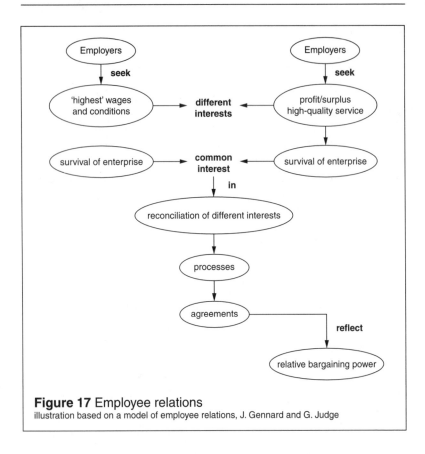

Figure 17 Employee relations
illustration based on a model of employee relations, J. Gennard and G. Judge

by European Union comparison the UK has dropped from the cluster of high density union countries, to the median cluster (Table 4).

Table 4 Clusters of Union Density

High		Median		Low	
Sweden	91%	Italy	44%	Portugal	26%
Denmark	80%	Luxembourg	43%	Netherlands	26%
Finland	79%	Austria	41%	Greece	24%
Belgium	52%	UK	33%	Spain	19%
Ireland	49%	Germany	29%	France	9%

Source: World Labour Report 1997–98, International Labour Organisation.

The trade union movement is facing the challenge of a rapidly changing world of work. Many of the old jobs have gone, to be replaced by jobs requiring new skills and working practices. The new service industries that have come to dominate the economy do not have a strong history of trade unionism, and those on part-time and temporary contracts are far less inclined to join trade unions. The dominance of the blue-collar workers (i.e. manual operatives) have been whittled away by the decline of manufacturing and the rise of white-collar services (i.e. people who largely work with Information and Communications Technology, and directly in customer servicing). Much of Britain's projected jobs growth is made up of part-time employment. Of Britain's six million part-time workers – 88 per cent of them women – only a quarter belong to a trade union.

At the same time, there are increasing numbers of people doing better paid jobs and enjoying a more 'middle class' lifestyle. Higher incomes have enabled more people to buy their own homes and to purchase shares in publicly listed companies. All these factors have helped to change people's attitudes towards trade unions, and have led to changes in the relative size and importance of various union groupings. Increasingly, employers are seeking '**single-union deals**' with only one union operating in an industrial unit.

Managerial perspectives of employee relations

Many commentators believe that trade unions are out of date. They associate unions with an era of confrontation in the 1970s which led to serious inflexibilities in the UK economy. During the 1980s and 1990s the development of new approaches in many areas of industry was largely based on a managerial perspective of the management of employee relations and of empowerment. Human Resource Management was at the forefront of this new development involving a range of measures known as Employee Involvement (EI). EI was all about creating the processes and agreements which would lead to shared interests in the workplace.

Unitary perspective

Human Resource Management is largely based on what is termed a 'unitary perspective' of employee relations. A unitary perspective involves all members of an organisation pulling in the same direction, i.e. towards the achievement of organisational objectives. This can only be successful where employees are committed to the organisation. A range of integrated processes therefore need to be established to gain commitment of the workforce. Typical activities involved in this integrated HRM package include:

- Teamwork. Employees work together, often in self-managing teams, taking shared responsibility for decision making. Within a team there.
- Empowerment. The devolving of decision making to lower levels in the organisation.
- **Appraisal schemes**. Team members will meet at regular intervals with their team leader to discuss and agree performance targets. This will involve looking at previous performance and considering future performance.
- Part of the function of the appraisal process will be to tie in the development needs of individual employees with the overarching objectives of the organisation.
- **Team briefings**. Regular meetings will take place between managers, team leaders, and team members, in which everyone can be briefed about developments within the organisation, so that everyone can share information.
- **Performance-related reward systems**. Pay and other reward systems in the organisation will be tied to individual, group and organisational performance. Profit-related pay, and share ownership schemes are extensions of performance-related reward systems.
- **Communications systems**. Organisations will establish communication systems which enable employees to better understand the firms' objectives and its market standing (see Benetton agreement).

Benetton strikes communications agreement with unions

On 21 July 1999 Benetton struck an agreement with its three major trade unions to improve its international communications system. It will now inform employees of business related developments on an annual basis. The areas covered are:

- the economic situation of the textiles sector and market growth
- company policies, especially plans for international expansion and outsourcing
- business prospects for the company
- employment developments in Italy and abroad
- investment plans
- annual company results.

Criticisms of the unitary perspective

A number of dissenting voices have argued that the development of a **unitary** (managerial) **perspective** of employee relations is not necessarily good for employees or for employers.

Trade unions came into existence because employees were being exploited by unscrupulous employers and to provide a safety net of benefits for working class people in the UK.

Today, there are still many employees who are being exploited, and many would argue that the state does not provide benefits which are adequate to meet the basic needs of poor workers. New types of flexible work provide us with clear examples of exploitation. For example, young workers in the fast food industry work long hours, with low pay, and poor contractual arrangements. They are often seen as a disposable asset; one young person can quickly be replaced by another.

Some people therefore favour a pluralist perspective of human relations. This view recognises that there are a number of stakeholders in an organisation with different standpoints. These differences should not be ignored. The successful organisation will welcome diversity and seek ways of managing this diversity in an effective and productive way.

The development of call centres

The development of **call centres** in the UK (where an employee works with a telephone and a computer screen, e.g. in telephone banking) have been cited as illustrating some of the worst business practices. Employees are often employed on very short-term contracts and are expected to engage in emotionally draining relationships with telephone clients. Call centre operators are expected to 'smile down the telephone line' and their work is closely monitored by supervisors using computer monitoring systems. Fernie and Metcalfe (1997) describe the nature of such practices in the following way: 'The possibilities for monitoring behaviour and measuring output are amazing to behold – the tyranny of the assembly line is but a Sunday School picnic compared with the control that management can exercise in computer telephony.' It is estimated that 2.3 per cent of all UK workers will be working in call centres by 2002.

Flexible conditions can also be criticised from an employer's point of view because they do not encourage a '**commitment model**' of employee relations. Part-time, short-term contracted labour will have very little commitment to the employing organisation, and the organisation will have all the extra costs of continual recruitment, selection and training.

Processes and agreements will need to be negotiated which:

- recognise and find ways of reconciling a plurality of interests
- create working agreements with are welcomed by all parties
- accept that conflict is normal, and that conflict needs to be successfully managed through bargaining processes leading to agreements.

Reconciling different interests

A key difference in interest between employers and employees is over the price at which employees sell their labour and the terms under which employees are prepared to work. There are all sorts of issues to be considered including pay, hours of work, paid holidays, sick pay schemes, incentive schemes, pension arrangements, child care facilities, job security, etc.

There are all sorts of trade-offs that will be involved in arriving at agreements covering working conditions and terms. For example, if employers want employees to adopt flexible arrangements such as multi-skilling, they will usually have to offer better terms and conditions. If employers want to employ highly productive high quality employees, then they will have to make a range of attractive offers including incentive schemes, child care arrangements, etc.

The different interests of employers and employees are usually reconciled through a negotiating process to create agreements. This usually involves identifying the common ground in each other's positions. The most common types of negotiation are as follows:

1. **Bargaining** – involves trade-offs within a list of demands made by the two parties.
2. **Grievance handling** – to resolve complaints (usually by employees).
3. **Group problem solving** where the employer sets out the details of areas where employees will co-operate. Management requests assistance in obtaining information to help solve the identified problem.

Employee relations processes

Typical employee relations processes involve the following:

- Unilateral action

Unilateral action is where management directly imposes changes to employees' terms and conditions. There is evidence that this approach has become more common with the decline in power of trade unions.

- Joint consultation

Joint consultation involves managers consulting employees and their representative prior to making a decision. In the last two decades of the twentieth cen-tury there was a decline in the number of formal joint consultative processes as the number of Works Councils decreased because the types of industries in which they were typically found were in decline.

- Collective bargaining

Collective bargaining is the process through which representatives of employers (employers' organisations) and employees (trade unions) come together to make joint agreements on behalf of (often) large numbers of employees. Collective bargaining went into serious decline in the 1980s and 1990s with the decline of trade unions.

- Third-party intervention

The Advisory, Conciliation and Arbitration Service (ACAS) was set up by the UK government in 1974 in order to improve industrial relations by offering **third-party intervention**. It is managed by a council of nine members; three chosen by the TUC, three chosen by the Confederation of British Industry (CBI) and three who are independent. In industrial relations issues, where there is deadlock, the parties may ask ACAS to help. ACAS may come up with a binding solution or just make recommendations.

Conciliation involves keeping the two sides talking, and hopefully through negotiation to arrive at a solution to a dispute. **Arbitration** takes the form of an award made after the arbitrators have heard the cases of the parties involved in the dispute.

The number of cases of third-party involvement in employee relations has fallen substantially over the years, partly because a number of cases created precedents and guidelines which have been more widely interpreted in the course of time.

- Industrial sanctions

The main sanctions available to employers include the relocation of activity to another site, the locking out of the workforce, or dismissal of staff involved in industrial action. Employees have available a range of possible sanctions including: the 'go slow', **'working to rule'** (only doing work which is officially set out in the contract of employment and other work rules), a 'selective strike' (covering selected aspects of work, or selected groups of employees – to have maximum impact), or an 'all-out strike' (involving all activities and the total unionised workforce). Clearly, **industrial sanctions** are last resort measures designed to have the maximum impact on the other party.

The UK was notorious for its poor industrial relations during the 1970s. Since then there has been a dramatic fall in strike and other activity, largely as a result of the demise of the unions and the growth of managerial Human Resource Management perspectives.

Agreements

The processes of employee relations will lead to agreement about employment relationships, terms and conditions of work. These agreements may be of a collective nature (covering a group of employees) or of an individual nature (a personal contract). Interestingly, collective agreements are not legally binding in the UK – they are binding in honour only. Increasingly, agreements are made by personal contracts, and as already been seen (Chapter 4), the success of human relations policies depends on the creation of a psychological contract between employer and employee.

It is standard practice to classify agreements into two main groupings:

1. **Substantive agreements** cover monetary aspects such as pay, hours worked, holiday arrangements, etc.
2. **Procedural agreements** set out standards of conduct for employers and employees so as to lead to the peaceful reconciliation of interests.

Procedural agreements cover a broad range of issues such as grievances, disputes, dismissal, discipline, redundancy, job grading, health and safety, promotion, staff development, and career reviews.

Within a large organisation, for example Ford in the UK, agreements will be made at a number of levels – at a national level, at a plant level, or even within a specific group.

National agreements

In 1999 only 10 per cent of employees were directly affected by national agreements compared with 35 per cent in 1980. The advantage of national bargaining is that it creates minimum standards and curbs the excesses of the worst employers. However, pay rates negotiated at national level are usually very low and therefore will require a two-tier bargaining process to arrange locally negotiated supplements.

Power relations in the bargaining process

Relative power usually determines who comes out best from a bargaining process. While in recent years employer bargaining power has been enhanced by the decline in unionisation, both employers and trade unions have had to bow to the growing power of the customer in the modern market economy, both in the public and private sectors.

While unskilled, routinised labour continues to have little industrial muscle, the new knowledge workers have considerable power. Therefore the most widespread application of managerial Human Resource Management initiatives has been to knowledge workers, whose knowledge and skills drive today's modern successful organisations. Knowledge workers have therefore received the highest pay awards, the best perks, terms and conditions, as well as enjoying the most secure employment, the greatest levels of empowerment, and so on.

Marchington (1982) sets out that management needs to consider four questions in identifying the power of a particular work group:

1. Does the group have the capacity to inflict substantial costs on the organisation?
2. Is the group aware that it has that capacity?
3. Does the group have experience of using its power against the organisation?
4. What was the outcome of the use of that bargaining power?

Groups that can inflict costs on the organisation, know that they can do it, and have used that power successfully in the past are clearly in the strongest position to get what they want. It is not surprising that HRM approaches are used widely with such groups.

The way forward for employee relations

The 1990s was a period in which managers increasingly sought to use the Human Resource Management approach to employee relations by imposing management agendas onto the employment relationship. Faced by a loss of membership, unions resorted to a series of mergers, and a refocus on developing the service function of unions (i.e. in providing a range of services and benefits to members).

Increasingly employee relations became fragmented. For example, in the National Health Service, as the service was broken down into self-managing trusts, employee relations were increasingly carried out at a local level between the unions (Unison and the MSF) and local employers. Instead of bargaining taking place at a national level it increasingly took place between local officers (branch officials) and local managers. The local union officers increasingly took on a servicing role rather than developing a more participative union structure. Between 1974 and 1997 membership of Unison fell by 6 per cent and the MSF by 18 per cent. Changes in the National Health Service resulted in a downward shift of management, with general managers increasingly taking responsibility for budgets and performance measures. This led to a range of local and unit based efficiency savings including the spread of labour flexibility arrangements. Employee relations were increasingly dominated by the management agenda, while union representatives became primarily concerned with the task of limiting the adverse consequences for members of the implementation of policies aimed at achieving changes in the skill mix of employees, labour flexibility and the introduction of new work patterns. Both employers and employee representatives have found themselves increasingly having to perform to the standards required, by a third key stakeholder in the process, the consumer.

There is a very real danger that the voice of the worker in employee relationships is being subjugated to other interests. Where employees have no direct ownership of the decision making process in the workplace they may increasingly feel alienated from 'real' decision making, leading to low morale and low motivation.

Managerial perspectives of Human Resource Management tend towards the unitarist rather than the pluralist view of employee relationships. In contrast the notion of Social Partnership is concerned with genuine employee participation in decision making – where employees and their representatives help to shape the agenda.

The European Works Council Directive (1994) goes some way to forcing organisations to become more participative. The Directive became operational in the UK in December 1999 and requires companies employing more than 1000 people in the member states and at least 150 employees in each of any two member states to start negotiations on setting up a **European Works Council** if employees ask them to do so. This Directive covers between 100 and 200 major companies in the UK.

This means that companies have to set up a consultation system with their employees' representatives, most likely, though not necessarily, with their trade unions. The firm would have a duty to consult on issues such as employment conditions, plant relocation, and mergers. Advantages to employers of having a Works Council in place include improved motivation and employer relationships. Employees will understand the firm's objectives and problems, and have an opportunity to participate in the framing of objectives and the solving of problems.

In the early 2000s many trade unionists are placing less emphasis on the 'service' view of the trade union (primarily to offer a range of financial services to members) and more emphasis on an 'organising' view of unions – whereby unions set out to encourage members to organise in the workplace so that groups of committed individuals work to encourage other members of the workforce to take responsibility for involvement in workplace issues. At the same time, unions are placing less emphasis on industrial action, and more on using legal frameworks to win improvements in working conditions (e.g. where the union supports employees in cases that they put before industrial tribunals). Also, governments, unions and employers are working more closely to develop social partnerships where these groupings work in closer collaboration to secure the long-term competitiveness and future of the organisation and hence the workforce.

KEY WORDS

Employee relations	Group problem solving
Union density	Unilateral action
Single-union deals	Joint consultation
Employee Involvement (EI)	Collective bargaining
Appraisal schemes	Third-party intervention
Team briefings	Conciliation
Performance-related reward systems	Arbitration
Unitary perspective	Working to rule
Call centres	Industrial sanctions
Commitment model	Substantive agreements
Bargaining	Procedural agreements
Grievance handling	European Works Council

Further reading

Cowling, A. and Mailer, C., Chapter 7 in *Managing Human Resources*, Arnold, 1998.

Foot, M. and Hook, C., Chapter 13 in *Introducing Human Resource Management*, Longman, 1999.

Dransfield, R. *et al.*, Chapters 16 and 17 in *Human Resource Management for Higher Awards*, Heinemann, 1996.

Gennard, J. and Judge, G., Chapter 2 in *Employee Relations*, Institute of Personnel and Development, 1997.

Further references

Carter, B. and Poynter, G., 'Union in a changing climate: MSF and Unison experiences in the new public sector', *Industrial Relations Journal*, Vol. 30, No. 5. Dec 1999, pp 499–513.

Fernie, S. and Metcalfe, D., '(Not) hanging on the telephone: payment systems in the new sweatshops'. Centre for Economic Performance, London School of Economics, 1997.

Marchington, M., *Managing Industrial Relations*. McGraw-Hill, (1982) Chapter 7.

Uncredited. 'Union Decline Bottoms Out'. *Labour Research Magazine*, August 1999.

Useful websites

Labour Research Department – produces the leaflet (eleven times a year), *Bargaining Report*, an account of developments in employee relations bargaining: www.lrd.org.UK

Trades Union Congress: www.tuc.org.uk/

Manufacturing, Science and Finance Union: www.msf.org.uk/

Essay topics

1. Do trade unions have any relevance to employee relations in the twenty-first century? [25 marks]
2. (a) How can managers best manage employee relations from a Human Resource Management perspective? [13 marks]
   (b) What would be the positive outcomes of effective management of this relationship? [12 marks]

Data response question

Read through the following data and then set out an assessment of the opportunities for unions to recruit new members in 2000 and beyond. [25 marks]

Opportunities for trade unions

Employees are most likely to join unions when three conditions are met:

1. They have a sense of grievance or injustice about their treatment in the workplace.
2. They believe that management is either to blame for their problem or is unwilling to deal fairly with it.
3. They believe that the union would be able to take effective action, which implies management would be willing to negotiate with the union.

Work related complaints reported to Citizens Advice Bureaux were a third higher in 2000 than they were in 1983.

Three-quarters of these complaints were by non-union employees, many of whom were women in the private services sector.

The ACAS annual report (1999) showed the following figures relating to claims for unfair dismissal at work:

1983	42 943
1987	40 817
1990	52 071
1993	75 181
1997	106 912

The British Social Attitudes Survey in 1997 showed that:

In 1983 – 30 per cent of employees agreed that the workplace was well managed.
In 1996 – the figure was 24 per cent.

In 1983 – 84 per cent of employees thought relations between management and employees at their workplace were 'very good' or 'quite good'.
In 1996 – the figure was 79 per cent.

In 1985 – the numbers of employees agreeing with the statement that: 'managers will always try to get the better of employees if given the chance' was 52 per cent.
In 1996 – the figure was 62 per cent.

The 1998 Workplace Employee Relations Survey showed that the majority of non-union members still believe unions are weak. Asked 'whether unions make a difference to what it is like at work', 28 per cent agreed with the statement.

In 1980 – half of Britain's new workplaces (under ten years old) were unionised.
In 2000 – only 18 per cent of Britain's new workplaces are unionised.

Compared with non-union counterparts, union members enjoy better pay and fringe benefits, enjoy more internal and 'off the job' training, are more likely to be consulted on workplace changes and are less likely to work long hours or be dismissed.

In a survey of managers in January 2000:

- 28 per cent of managers believed that unions help workplace performance
- 38 per cent of managers disagreed
- 72 per cent of managers preferred direct consultations with employees rather than consultations through a trade union.

Chapter Eight

Employment law

*'**Common law** is law that has been developed through the courts and which is based on past decisions. Generally speaking, the doctrine of precedent requires the courts to follow past decisions in cases with similar facts and covering the same points of law – although the doctrine of equity allows the courts in certain instances to reduce some of the harshness of the common law by looking at the fairness of the situation. **Statutory law** is created through an Act of Parliament (or statute) which then becomes binding on the courts. Today European Community legislation is given precedence over UK law in many situations.'*
Maureen Rawlinson

Human Resource Managers must have a good grasp of employment law. Employment law sets out the minimum standards that organisations must comply with in a range of areas concerning people at work. Of course, the 'good organisation' will always seek to do more than this required minimum. Effective organisations will always anticipate changes in the laws and make sure that they have put in place the policies and the practices long before the requirements appear on the statute books.

The ineffective organisation will think of compliance with the law as a cost to the business. However, this is short-sighted. By doing more than is required organisations will build a reputation as a 'good employer' and a 'good company'. The firm which always maintains legal requirements (and more) will never face the costs associated with prosecution (fines and other legal sanctions, bad press and poor publicity).

Contracts of employment

In law a contract exists when two parties reach an agreement which they both intend to be legally binding and under which both have an obligation.

Although the law does not require the contract to be made in writing, it does require a summary of the most important terms to be given to the employee – the **contract of employment** (Figure 18). The

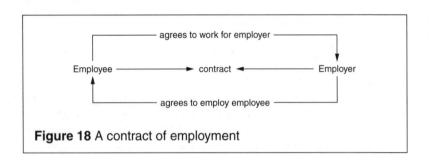

Figure 18 A contract of employment

Employment Rights Act (1996) sets out that the terms and conditions that must be set out in writing are:

- the names of the employer and employee
- the date when employment began
- whether the employment counts as a period of continuous employment with a previous employer, and the date of commencement of the previous employment where this is the case
- the scale or rate of pay and the method of calculating pay where the employee is paid by commission or bonus
- when payment is made (i.e. weekly or monthly), and the day or date of payment
- the hours to be worked, including any compulsory overtime
- holiday entitlement and holiday pay
- sick pay and injury arrangements
- entitlements to a pension scheme
- the length of notice of termination an employee must receive or give
- the job title
- the duration of temporary contracts
- the work location or locations
- any collective agreements that affect the job
- when the job requires work outside the UK for more than one month, the period of such work, the currency in which the employee will be paid and any other pay or benefits
- grievance procedures
- disciplinary procedures.

This information must be readily available to employees at all times.

Other statutory rights of employees

In addition to the contractual rights outlined above employees are also entitled by law to the following.

• An itemised pay statement

An itemised pay statement must set out the gross pay and the take-home pay with the amounts and reasons for any deductions.

• Notice of termination of employment

Both employer and employee are entitled to a minimum period of **notice of termination**. After a month's employment an employee must give at least a week's notice. An employer must give the employee (after a month's employment) at least one week's notice, rising to two weeks after two years of employment, three weeks after three years of employment, etc. up to a maximum of 12 weeks. However, in certain circumstances (see below) the employer is entitled to dismiss the employee.

• Written reasons for dismissal

Employees who have completed at least two years' continuous employment (before the date of termination) are entitled to receive, on request, from their employer, within 14 days, a written statement of the reasons for dismissal.

• Time off for public duties

People who hold posts such as that of magistrate, local councillor, and prison visitor are entitled to reasonable unpaid time off work to carry out these duties.

• Unfair dismissal

Employees have a statutory right not to be unfairly dismissed. There is also statutory provision for notice periods and severance pay.

The economic circumstances in which dismissal is regarded to be fair include when: the employer is ceasing, or intending to cease, business which employs workers; or that particular type of work ceases or has been reduced.

An employee can also be the subject of **fair dismissal** on account of their conduct – for example incapacity to perform tasks required, despite adequate warnings from the employer, serious or repeated incidents of misconduct or unauthorised absences, lateness, breaches of loyalty and refusing to obey orders (in each case reasonable warnings having been given).

Employees can be summarily dismissed for gross misconduct – theft, embezzlement, and acts of violence. A period of 28 days consultation prior to making the dismissal is the norm.

Examples of situations where dismissal would be regarded in law as being unfair would include dismissal for:

- trade union membership or activities or non-membership of a union
- pregnancy or other reasons concerned with maternity
- seeking to assert a legal right.

The limit on **unfair dismissal** awards was abolished in 1999, thus putting great pressure on organisations to make sure that they had in place adequate procedures for dismissing workers.

- ### Statutory Sick Pay
Employees have a right to **Statutory Sick Pay** (SSP) paid by the employer providing they meet certain requirements.

- ### Maternity rights
Pregnant employees are entitled to reasonable time off to keep appointments made on the advice of a registered medical practitioner, midwife or health visitor for antenatal care. A pregnant employee is entitled to 18 weeks' statutory maternity leave, whatever her length of service, although she must give the employer 21 days' written notice that she is pregnant and does not start maternity leave earlier than the eleventh week before the expected week of childbirth. A woman is entitled to **Statutory Maternity Pay** if she has worked for her employer for a continuous period of 26 weeks ending with the fifteenth week before the expected week of childbirth.

- ### Transfer of a business
If a business is transferred or sold to a new employer, then employees who are employed by the old employer are automatically transferred to become employees of the new employer.

- ### Shop working on Sundays
Workers in shops have the right not to be dismissed or picked out for redundancy or subject to any other sort of action as a result of refusing to work on a Sunday.

- ### Redundancy pay
Employees who are made redundant are entitled to receive a compensation payment, the amount of which is related to their age, weekly pay and length of service.

- ### Sex and race discrimination
The **Sex Discrimination Act** and the **Race Relations Act** have a number of similarities and because of this they are often interpreted in the same way by Industrial Tribunals. Both protect all employees

irrespective of age or status, whether they are full-time or part-time workers or have a fixed or temporary contract. They attempt to deal with three sorts of discrimination:

- direct discrimination
- indirect discrimination
- victimisation.

Direct discrimination occurs when one employee or candidate for a job is treated better or more favourably than another because of their race or sex, for example where two candidates with identical qualifications and experience apply for a job but one is not interviewed because of their sex or race.

Indirect discrimination takes place when all employees seem to be treated exactly the same on the surface, but when looked at more closely, members of a particular racial group or sex are found to be discriminated against. For example, an employer tries to insist that all female staff wear skirts. Clearly this will disadvantage groups whose culture or religion require that legs should be covered up. Until 2000 indirect discrimination was only illegal in the private sector – legislation is now being extended to cover the public sector as well.

Victimisation occurs when an employee is singled out for unfair treatment because they have attempted to exercise rights under the Race Relations Act, Sex Discrimination Act or Equal Pay Act, or have helped others to enforce their rights. For example, if an employee were to appear as a witness or to support another employee's claim for discrimination, and as a result was not chosen for promotion within an organisation, this would be classified as victimisation.

Discrimination

'A person discriminates against another if, on racial grounds, he treats another less favourably than he treats, or would treat, another person.'
The Race Relations Act, 1976

(The RRA defines discrimination on racial grounds as being based on colour, race, nationality or ethnic origin.)

'A person discriminates against a woman if, on the grounds of her sex he treats her less favourably than he treats a man.'
The Sex Discrimination Act, 1975

(The SDA applies equally to men and women.)

• Equal pay

The **Equal Pay Act** 1970 set out to ensure that women receive the same pay as men for the same or broadly similar work. If a woman (or man) wants to claim for pay discrimination she must ensure that whatever man she compares herself to is in the same employment, i.e. the man has to be employed by the same employer or an associated employer.

The purpose of the Equal Pay Act is to make sure that women are given the same treatment as men:

- who are engaged in like work in the same employment
- whose work is rated as equivalent
- whose work is otherwise of equal value.

Pay is defined under the Act as including:

- fringe benefits or the use of a car
- sick pay
- redundancies or severance pay
- the right to join a pension scheme.

• Disability discrimination

It is against the law for employers to discriminate against employees or prospective employees on account of disability. Small employers with less than 15 employees are not included.

The pay gap

Although the implementation of the Equal Pay Act led to a rapid narrowing of the gap between male and female earnings in the 1970s, since then the persistent **pay gap** has not narrowed despite women's gains in education and experience.

1999 figures showed that for every £1 and hour earned by men, women earned 81p.

Average earnings (£) of Britain's full time employees

	Hourly	Weekly	Annual
Women	8.7	326.5	16 481
Men	10.75	442.4	23 412
Pay gap (female as % of male)	80.9	73.8	70.4

Source: National Earnings Survey.

Employers may also have to make a 'reasonable adjustment' if their premises or working arrangements place a disabled person at a substantial disadvantage compared to a person without a disability.

The aim of the Act is to ensure that a disabled person is treated fairly. In effect, the Act seeks to ensure that a disability should not bar a person from employment or promotion unless it would really prevent them from doing the job and there is nothing the employer can reasonably do to overcome difficulties. A person who feels that they have been the subject of **disability discrimination** can complain to an Employment Tribunal. There is no ceiling to the compensation that can be awarded by the Tribunal.

- Working hours and annual leave

The working time regulations enforce the **European Working Time Directive** which came into force in the UK on 1 October 1999.

The legislation imposes a statutory right to a maximum working week of 48 hours for many workers, although this can be averaged out over 17 weeks, so there is room for some flexibility, but there are strict rules governing the regulation of night workers (limited to an average of 8 hours in each 24-hour period) and there are changes to the hours for young workers.

Workers who want to exceed the limit can make a written agreement to do so with their employees. The regulation also incorporates the Annual Leave Directive which gives all workers the right to a minimum of four weeks' paid annual leave).

Working Time Regulations: a major cost for the NHS

Nurses' holiday pay until recently was calculated on a lower basic rate that did not take into account their overtime payments and unsocial hours. However, the Working Time Directive stated that holiday pay for annual leave entitlement, which is four weeks per year, must be at the average weekly pay. The cost to the NHS of complying with this requirement is estimated to work out at £400m per year.

Publicans win test case over working hours

JEAN EAGLESHAM

Two publicans have won a settlement of claims that they were unfairly required to work more than 48 hours a week, in a case that suggests most middle managers are covered by the working time regulations.

Lawyers yesterday warned that a recent government amendment in this area could trigger a wealth of litigation against employers.

Bass Leisure Retail initially decided to fight the claim brought by William Marshall and Christopher Mortlock, two Birmingham licensees, on the basis the men were 'managing executives' and so exempt from the 48-hour-a-week limit. The publicans' union argued this exemption was aimed at a small band of people at the very top of companies only.

Bass has now in effect conceded this point. 'We're working on the principle that managers are covered. Obviously they have the right to opt out of the 48-hour limit, but that will be entirely up to the individuals,' said Bob Cartwright, communications director.

The Financial Times, 22 February 2000

The regulations cover the majority of workers (i.e. those covered by a contract of employment and agency and temporary workers, as well as freelance workers). They do not cover the self-employed, nor do they include workers in transport, sea fishing, other work at sea and doctors in training.

- Parental leave

From December 1999 parents have been entitled to 13 weeks' **parental leave** for each child. The employee's rights to take the leave last until the child's fifth birthday or until five years have elapsed following placement in the case of adoption. Parents of disabled children are able to use their leave over a longer period, up until the child's eighteenth birthday. The employee remains employed while on parental leave and at the end of the leave period is guaranteed the right to return to the same job as before.

- National Minimum Wage

The **National Minimum Wage** applies to most adult workers in the UK. In 1999 the standard rate was set at £3.60 an hour which applied to workers aged over 22 unless they were involved in accredited training, when the rate was £3.20 an hour for the first six months of the new job after which they received the standard rate. For workers aged 18 to 21 the rate was £3.00 per hour. By February 2000 the government announced a rise in the standard rate to £3.70 an hour from October 2000. The youth rate was set to rise from £3.00 to £3.20 from June 2000. Many Labour MPs would like to see the Minimum Wage being increased every year. A number of trade unions in 2000 felt that the Minimum Wage was too low and should be raised to at least £5.00 an hour.

Employers should know that:

- they are required by law to make sure their workers receive at least the National Minimum Wage
- they need to keep sufficient records to prove they are doing this
- they may be required by the workers, the Inland Revenue, an Employment Tribunal or a civil court to provide evidence to prove they are complying
- in a dispute the burden is on employers to prove they have complied
- employers who fail to comply can be required to pay arrears
- employers can be fined for failing to keep proper records
- it is against the law to sack or victimise a worker because of the Minimum Wage.

• Health and safety requirements

At common law an employer has a general duty to take reasonable care to avoid injury, disease or death occurring to employees at work.

Employers must:

- provide a safe place of work with safe means of getting in and out
- provide and maintain safe appliances and equipment and plant for carrying out work tasks
- provide and maintain a safe system of work
- provide competent people to carry out the work (thus the need for effective training).

An employer who is in breach of any of these duties can be sued by employees who are injured in any way. Employees are under a duty to take reasonable care for their own health and safety and that of others and to co-operate with their employer in carrying out health and safety duties.

All employers of more than five people must prepare written health and safety policy statements setting out health and safety arrangements and intentions. Every employer must carry out an assessment of health and safety risks of their employees and persons not employed by the organisation who might be at risk.

- **Termination of employment**
Except where an employee has been contracted to work just for a specific fixed period of times (or there are other circumstances written into the contract that automatically end it) employment can only be terminated by the employee or employer by giving a period of notice.

The contract can set out the period of notice required, and the only legal control is that the statutory minimum period of notice must be applied, i.e. one week for every completed year of employment up to a maximum of 12 weeks' notice.

An employer who dismisses someone without notice will be in breach of contract and liable to pay compensation. This is termed 'wrongful dismissal' and usually the employer's liability is limited to payment of salary in lieu of the notice that should have been given.

The European Union and UK employment law

In recent years many of the changes to UK employment laws have resulted from the need to apply European Union law:

- **European Union regulations** override domestic law.
- **European Union directives** have to be implemented through national law, e.g. the Working Time Directive.

The UK government and UK employment law

The Conservative government 1979–97 introduced a number of changes in the law which created greater flexibility in labour markets, e.g. by making it easier for employers to dismiss employees, and measures which weakened the legal protection of trade unions. While the current Labour government (1997–) is in favour of labour market flexibility it has also sought to develop fairness at work and to develop a partnership approach between employers and employees. Whereas the Conservatives opted out of the European Union's **Social Chapter** (which gave considerable rights to employees), Labour has signed up, leading to a raft of changes under the Employment Relations Act (1999).

KEY WORDS

Common Law	Indirect discrimination
Statutory Law	Victimisation
Contract of employment	Equal Pay Act
Itemised pay statement	Pay gap
Notice of termination	Disability discrimination
Fair dismissal	European Working Time
Unfair dismissal	Directive
Statutory Sick Pay	Parental leave
Statutory Maternity Pay	National Minimum Wage
Sex Discrimination Act	European Union regulations
Race Relations Act	European Union directives
Direct discrimination	Social Chapter

Further reading

Needham, D. *et al.*, Chapter 24 in *Business for Higher Awards*, Heinemann Educational, 1999.

Dransfield, R. *et al.*, Chapter 13 in *Human Resource Management for Higher Awards*, Heinemann, 1996.

Foot, M. and Hook, C., Chapter 6 in *Introducing Human Resource Management*, Longman, 1999.

Fairness at Work, Government White Paper, May 1998 (available on Internet at www.dti.gov.uk/IR/fairness/fore.htm).

Useful websites

Acts of Parliament: www.hmso.gov.uk/acts.htm

Briefing articles about a range of recent laws; type in 'employment rights' to find articles about relevant legal changes: www.lawrite.co.uk

European Union Law, and UK law online: www.leeds.ac.uk//hamlyn/european.htm

Health and Safety Executive: www.open.gov.uk/hse/hsehome.htm

Essay topics

1. Complying with employment legislation generally adds to the employer's costs.
   (a) Should employers therefore view increases in employment laws in a negative light? [12 marks]
   (b) Are there any benefits to employers of doing more than is required by employment legislation? [13 marks]

2. (a) To what extent have recent changes in employment law benefited the employee at the expense of the employer? [12 marks]
   (b) How might this have negative impacts for the UK economy? [13 marks]

Data response question
Study the following information on the Employment Relations Act, 1999. Then answer the questions below.

The Employment Relations Act, 1999

Some of the key measures in the Employment Relations Act included the following:

- Measures to help parents combine home and work responsibilities.
- Increasing maternity leave for all employees to 18 weeks.
- 40 weeks' maternity leave after one year, rather than two.
- Three months' unpaid parental leave, including for adoptive parents.
- The right to take time off for domestic emergencies.
- Tackling discrimination against part-time workers.
- Minimum standards for all individuals at work.
- Raising the limits on compensatory awards for unfair dismissal to £50 000.
- Extending protection against dismissal for those taking lawfully organised industrial action.
- Prohibiting unfair dismissal waivers in fixed-term contracts.
- The right for workers to be accompanied by a fellow worker or union official at disciplinary or grievance hearings.
- Prohibiting 'blacklisting' or other discrimination because of union membership.
- A statutory procedure for individuals to obtain recognition for trade unions, where there is clear support for this.
- Legislation to improve the regulation of employment agencies, and to better protect the interests of those using them.

1. How might the Employment Relations Act impact on the powers of trade unions in this country? What are the likely impacts of this change in powers for:
   (a) business organisations
   (b) union membership and recruitment
   (c) employee relations? [9 marks]

2. (a) Which of the changes outlined above are likely to prove to be most costly for employing organisations? [4 marks]

   (b) How might they therefore react to the new legislation? [4 marks]

3. (a) What do you see as being the government's overall intention in introducing the Employment Relations Act? [3 marks]

   (b) What do you think the major impact of the new Act will be? [5 marks]

Conclusion

Contrasting views on HRM

Human Resource Management has been a popular managerial perspective in recent years, although as this book has shown, there is considerable debate as to what HRM really means. To some people it is simply a set of managerial approaches designed to bring people and their actions in line with the requirements of corporate strategies and objectives. If this view is correct, then we have not moved very far forward from the days of Ford and Taylor. A contrasting view is that HRM is all about liberating individuals that work for an organisation, by giving them opportunities to take a genuine responsibility for their own personal development, and to work with the organisation to achieve shared objectives.

The challenge facing business organisations today

Business organisations are faced with a dilemma. Because they operate in a competitive environment, they need to be responsive, and this can be best achieved through the adoption of flexible HRM solutions, requiring a 'caring approach'. However, at the same time they are faced by a competitive business environment which often demands restructuring initiatives, which often means the cutting out of non-essential labour through downsizing.

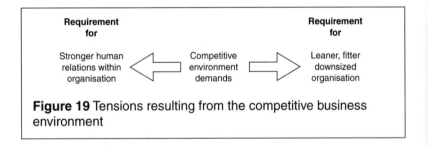

Figure 19 Tensions resulting from the competitive business environment

The net result is that business organisations may often appear to be hypocritical. While they 'talk up' HRM initiatives they often engage in what are perceived to be ruthless downsizing activities.

A typical example of this occurred at Rover in the Spring of 2000. In the late 1990's the takeover of Rover by BMW had been wel-

We won't go quietly, say 80,000 Rover workers

Cole Moreton

THE BANNER was bold. 'Tony Blair – if we lose our jobs, you'll lose yours.' Just behind it, among the 80,000 marchers assembled in the centre of Birmingham yesterday, was an effigy of the Prime Minister in BMW overalls. Someone was stabbing him in the back with a cardboard axe, a sign of the betrayal felt by many of those present.

This was the biggest demonstration in Birmingham since the 1970s – and the largest mass protest since the days when the miners took on the Thatcher government.

At the Masshouse Circus assembly point there was no escaping the symbolism of the skyline: cranes, factory chimneys and gas towers bearing witness to the place of heavy industry, and car manufacturing in particular; as foundation stones of West Midlands life. The fear that drove people of all ages on to the streets was that if BMW sells Rover; as it plans to, up to 50,000 workers could lose their jobs. Not just at the Longbridge plant, whose workers turned out *en masse*, but at many other businesses that depend on supplying the manufacturer, or on the workers spending their wages.

'When the docks closed, Liverpool was decimated, and it ain't got over it yet,' said Bob Jones, of King's Norton. 'The people of Birmingham don't want to go through that. They just want to go on as they are but, if you wake us up like this, the march will just be the start.'

Bill Morris, the general secretary of the TGWU, which organised the march, said: 'BMW has accepted the hospitality of the West Midlands community and then decided it should just walk away. It has to accept that it has some responsibility.'

Sometimes such marches have a carnival atmosphere, as families come together to make their point and find themselves smiling at the unfamiliarity of protesting in the street. Not yesterday. The bagpipes were mournful.

However, Tony Woodley, a TGWU negotiator who has been talking to BMW, promised: 'We're not going quietly, we are united to tell them they've got to negotiate a deal that we, the workers and the British public, are ready to accept – not the sellout that's on the table. Until we get that, Mr BMW, you will get no peace.'

The Independent on Sunday, 2 April, 2000

comed in the West Midlands, and employees had responded positively to new initiatives including changes involving teamworking, multiskilling and the empowerment of production line operatives to take on more responsibility for operational decision making.

However, by the turn of the new millennium Rover was struggling, with huge stockpiles of unsold vehicles as a result of the high pound, the strength of competition in the industry, and an unfavourable demand for the product. When BMW decided to pull out, the largest industrial protest in this country since the 1980's was seen.

The cynicism expressed by Rover workers is symptomatic of a more widespread distrust of the management agenda which has been prevalent in some quarters of the British industrial scene in recent times, for example, in banking with the development of telephone and online banking services to replace traditional banking (with the replacement of full time bank employees with short term contract workers operating from call centres).

The challenge facing management in modern organisations therefore is to create an 'inclusive organisation' in which employees feel party to decision making processes, and in which there is a shared understanding of the change process, which seeks to avoid exploitation and the treatment of employees as 'disposable assets'. The reality of a modern flexible economy is that change is inevitable, and that loyalty is no guarantee of secure employment. However, employees have the right to full information about the likelihood of change in the organisation, and why these changes are necessary.

In April 1994, Greg Dyke, the director general of the BBC, addressed the corporation's 23,000 staff to explain his plans to make the organisation happier and ' "more inclusive" '. He explained that he would be replacing the hierarchical structures of his predecessor (John Birt) with a new organisational structure which he likened to a flower, based on a number of petals (including for example a petal including drama productions). However, at the same time as outlining his plans for a more human structure to relationships within the corporation, he made it clear that there would be a number of cost savings, including large scale job losses, and a number of cost savings (such as the crackdown on the provision of taxis for staff working anti-social hours).

The changing industrial relations environment

From 1979 onwards in the United Kingdom, the employee relations agenda was increasingly steered by management. It remains to be seen whether trade unions will begin to regain some of the ground they lost in the period 1979–97, and the impact that this might have on flexible working practices. During the 80's and 90's business organisations increasingly adopted the flexible models which have been so successful in creating new (but different) jobs in the United States.

Dyke axes chauffeurs for senior BBC executives

JANE ROBINS

CHAUFFEUR-DRIVEN cars for senior BBC executives are to go in a management restructuring announced yesterday by the director general, Greg Dyke. The shake-up reverses many management systems put in place by his predecessor, Lord Birt.

Expensive cars and drivers for top BBC administrators were seen as symbolic of the old regime, accused of rewarding managers ahead of programme makers. The purge on perks forms part of an enormous cost-cutting drive expected to yield savings of £200m a year for the corporation from next year, helping the BBC to achieve a government savings target of £1.2bn over seven years.

'People on the BBC executive don't yet know this, but they won't be getting chauffeured cars,' said Mr Dyke, with some of the executive members present and looking slightly glum at the announcement.

He said he wanted to scrap a system that allowed some executives to have two company cars, and said the use of taxis by staff would be reduced. Mr Dyke himself brought a six-year-old Jaguar with him from his previous job at Pearson and has a BBC driver.

He said hundreds of jobs would be scrapped over the coming months to reduce the duplication of functions. Strategy departments, which have proliferated throughout the BBC, are to be replaced by one central strategy group. The BBC's many press and public relations departments will also be rationalised.

Mr Dyke said his restructuring should mean that about 85 per cent of BBC money should, within five years, be spent on programmes rather than the current 76 per cent. The change was essential because the BBC was in a position of financial decline within the British broadcasting market. He would aim to restructure the corporation, putting programme makers at the centre of the corporation and cutting out a layer of management introduced by Lord Birt. His controversial broadcast and production departments would be abolished in many areas including sports, children's and education programming.

Mr Dyke also announced the scrapping of the BBC's corporate centre and policy and planning unit, which staff dubbed the Birt 'thought police'. He also said the cumbersome performance review process introduced by Lord Birt would be cut 'drastically'.

The new structure is 'flatter, more inclusive, and will result in more collaboration and less internal competition; more leadership and less management', Mr Dyke said. Last week, he said that the BBC was 'massively over-managed and under-led', a comment seen as an attack on Lord Birt's regime.

Mr Dyke also plans to put more money into in-house programme production. Lord Birt presided over the loss of many talented BBC programme makers who set up their own independent companies, sometimes with guarantees of many years' work from the BBC. 'People have walked out of here with guaranteed production for the next few years,' Mr Dyke told staff. 'Those days are over.'

The Independent, 4 April 2000

Challenges to the individual in a flexible labour market

Many people today recognise the importance of regularly updating their skills, knowledge, and attitudes in relation to the world of work, and relationships in the workplace. The concept of lifelong learning involves individuals continuously identifying areas for personal development and training, and then seeking ways of improving their portfolio of skills in order to become more 'employable'.

A two way pscyhological contract

References have been made in a number of sections of this text to the importance of the psychological contract between the employing organisation and the individual employee. Psychological contracting is the process of arriving at a shared understanding between the organisation and the individual, as to obligations involved in the employment relationship. For effective HRM, it is essential that this process is absolutely clear and that both parties are familiar with potential changes in the business (for example, a fall in profits for the business) and social environment (for example, a change in the personal circumstances of an individual) which may affect the contract.

Peter Herriot and Carole Pemberton present a useful model of the stages of psychological contracting which alert us to the fact that the organisation's want and the individual's wants can change, requiring ongoing renegotiation of the contract. It would be naive to assume that a psychological contract once established would be set in stone.

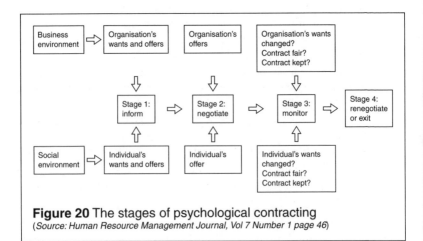

Figure 20 The stages of psychological contracting
(*Source: Human Resource Management Journal, Vol 7 Number 1 page 46*)

The state of the labour market

In 2000 it appears that the labour market is healthier in a number of respects than it was in the mid-1990's, although the government (as ever) has been accused of massaging the employment statistics. A Treasury report published on 29 February 2000 showed that, whereas in 1990 two-thirds of unemployed people lived in areas where there were more than ten applicants for every job available, only 2 per cent faced such competition in 2000. However, even people in this 'tail' of deprived areas where the immediate job prospects are less promising do not live more than a few miles from employment opportunities. 'Almost without exception, areas of high unemployment lie within easy travelling distance of areas where vacancies are plentiful', the report stated. The current Labour government has therefore pushed ahead with its employment policy of encouraging people to become more flexible and to take responsibility for gaining employment in order to remove a dependency culture.

UK policy is echoed on a wider scale in the European Union where the importance of flexibility has been more widely accepted. For example, the 1998 European Union 'Jobs Summit' under the Luxembourg Presidency of the Council of Ministers put forward a number of proposals to improve work opportunities in the European Union:

- employability. Member states were urged to offer employability measures (such as training, retraining or work experience) to all young unemployed people within 6 months of them becoming unemployed, and to all adults within 12 months. Particular attention was to be given to the long-term unemployed
- entrepreneurship. The setting up and running of businesses is to be encouraged – e.g. by easing the tax and administrative burdens on small and medium sized enterprises
- adaptability. The key work is flexibility, with member states recommended to investigate the legal bases of employment contracts and to encourage new forms that encourage job security coupled with adaptability – i.e. to find new forms of the flexible work organisation
- equal opportunities. A higher participation of women in the workforce is to be encouraged e.g. through child care provision and making sure that employers comply with laws on part-time work, parental leave, and career breaks.

However, the late 1990's also saw the passage of a number of new laws including the Employment Relations Act, which provide greater social protection to employees including the flexible workforce, but which may serve to reduce the flexibility of UK labour markets.

Those that see HRM as being part of a management plot to cut costs while seeking to maintain workforce compliance, point to the human cost of the widescale delayering processes that took place at the end of the 20th century. There are many voices that felt that this process went too far. For example, in May 1996, there was considerable alarm at the comments of Wall Street economist, Stephen Roach, the chief economist at Morgan Stanley, one of America's biggest investment banks. As an early advocate of downsizing and delayering he then went on to have serious reservations:

> 'For years I have extolled the virtues of America's productivity-led recovery,' he wrote in a circular to clients. 'I must confess I am now having second thoughts. These doubts have caused me to rethink many of the glorious consequences that I have long argued would be forthcoming.... Tactics of open-ended downsizing and real wage compression are ultimately recipes for industrial extinction.'

Roach's point was that downsizing was fine, if companies were making room for genuine performance improvements. However, the evidence was that downsizing and stripping out layers of employees had become a strategy in itself – one which was (and is) destroying the trust of employees based on a notion of the psychological contract.

A key aspect of Human Resource Management has been the concept of giving line managers increased responsibility for HRM related work, using the support network and systems provided by the central HRM function. This approach has been enthusiastically championed by those that want to see HRM spread across the organisation, coupled with a prominent part in corporate objectives and plans. While much has been written about this approach, there is considerable evidence that using line managers as the prime vehicle for HRM has not been successful across the board. The idea is widely 'talked up' but rarely achieved in practice, largely because insufficient organisational resources (including training) have not been made available to make HRM a reality (McGovern, 1999; Cunningham, 1999).

The success of HRM in the next few years will depend on the extent to which organisations are prepared to commit themselves to their people by developing integrated approaches based on a genuine belief in the mutual development of the organisation, and of the individuals that make up that organisation. What is clear is that the best chance for the success of HRM initiatives will occur within a framework of work security, trust, and equality of opportunity. Whether these conditions will be created in an environment dominated by managerial perspectives remains to be seen.

Further references

Cunningham, I. and Hyman, J., 'Devolving human resource responsibilities to the line'. *Personal Review*, Vol. 28, N. 1/2 1999.

Herriot, P. and Pemberton, C., 'Facilitating new deals'. *Human Resource Management Journal*, Vol. 7, No. 1. 1999.

McGovern, P. *et al.*, 'Human Resource Management on the line?'. *Human Resource Management Journal*, Vol. 7, No. 4. 1999.

Index